Content

The Law and Tradition as they affect Walking in Scotland; Scotland's Hills and Mountains: a Concordat; Glossary of Gaelic Names; Safety on the Hills; Useful Organisations; Ordnance Survey Maps

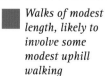

Short, easy walks

Walks of modest length, likely to involve some modest uphill walking

More challenging walks which may be longer and/or over more rugged terrain, often with some stiff climbs

Keymap

pathfinder® guide

Loch Lomond, Trossachs, Stirling *and* Clackmannan

WALKS

*Compiled by
John Brooks,
Neil Coates and
Brian Conduit*

JARROLD
publishing

Acknowledgements
With thanks to Hamish Brown, Chris and John Harvey, Mr P.M.
Fairweather of Argyll Estates, the officers of Loch Awe, Cowal,
and Aberfoyle Forest Districts, and all others who gave help and
advice. Thanks also to Brenda Stroud who supplied valuable
information used in the preparation of this new edition.

Text:	John Brooks, Brian Conduit, Neil Coates
	Revised text for 2004 edition, Hugh Taylor
Photography:	John Brooks, Brian Conduit, Neil Coates
Editorial:	Ark Creative, Norwich
Design:	Ark Creative, Norwich

Series Consultant: Brian Conduit

Jarrold Publishing   ISBN 0-7117-2225-0

First published 1992 by Jarrold Publishing and Ordnance Survey
Revised and reprinted 1995, 1997, 2002, 2004.

Printed in Belgium
by Proost NV, Turnhout. 5/04

Jarrold Publishing
Pathfinder Guides, Whitefriars, Norwich NR3 1TR
E-mail: info@totalwalking.co.uk
www.totalwalking.co.uk

Front cover: Castle Campbell
Previous page: Loch Lomond and Arrochar Alps from Ptarmigan

Keymap

At-a-glance...

Walk	Page	Start	Nat. Grid Reference	Distance	Time	Highest Point
Ancient Forest below Beinn Dubhchraig	44	Near Tyndrum	NN 344291	6½ miles (10.5km)	4 hrs	1,509ft (460m)
Beinn Tharsuinn and Beinn Lochain	61	Lettermay, Lochgoilhead	NN 188002	7 miles (11.3km)	5½ hrs	2,031ft (619m)
Ben A'an	34	Near the Trossachs Hotel	NN 510509	2 miles (3.2km)	1½ hrs	1,491ft (454m)
Ben Cleuch	82	Alva Glen	NS 885975	7½ miles (12.1km)	5 hrs	2,365ft (721m)
Ben Ledi	48	Corriechrombie bridge, nr. Callander	NN 586092	6 miles (9.7km)	3½ hrs	2,883ft (879m)
Ben Lomond from Rowardennan	78	Rowardennan	NS 359986	7½ miles (12.1km)	5 hrs	3,194ft (974m)
Ben More and Stob Binnein	86	Glen Dochart	NN 456275	10 miles (16.1km)	8 hrs	3,851ft (1174m)
Ben Venue	46	Loch Achray hotel	NN 505063	6 miles (9.7km)	4 hrs	2,306ft (703m)
Ben Vorlich (Loch Earn)	64	Advorlich, on south side of Loch Earn	NN 633232	7 miles (11.3km)	5½ hrs	3,231ft (985m)
Brack, The	67	Ardgartan Tourist Information Centre	NN 269037	9½ miles (15.3km)	5 hrs	2,391ft (727m)
Cobbler, The	71	Head of Loch Long	NN 294048	7 miles (11.3km)	6 hrs	2,900ft (884m)
Conic Hill and Balmaha	53	On the West Highland Way	NS 479906	9½ miles (15.3km)	4½ hrs	1,148ft (350m)
Cruach Ardrain	75	Glen Falloch, near Crianlarich	NN 369239	7½ miles (12.1km)	6 hrs	3,428ft (1046m)
Dollar Glen and Glenquey Reservoir	30	Dollar Glen, from A91	NS 962990	5 miles (8km)	2½ hrs	984ft (300m)
Donich Water and Lochgoilhead	16	Lochgoilhead	NN 200016	2½ miles (4km)	1½ hrs	459ft (140m)
Doune Hill	39	Glenmollochan, at head of Glen Luss	NS 332941	7½ miles (12.1km)	5 hrs	2,408ft (734m)
Dumyat	24	North of Bridge of Allan	NS 813980	3 miles (4.8km)	2 hrs	1,373ft (418m)
Dunblane and Bridge of Allan	42	Dunblane, Cathedral Square	NN 782014	6 miles (9.7km)	3 hrs	230ft (70m)
Fault Trail, The	26	David Marshall Lodge	NN 520014	3 miles (4.8km)	2½ hrs	1,017ft (310m)
Gartmorn Dam	22	Gartmorn Dam Country Park	NS 912940	3 miles (4.8km)	1½ hrs	183ft (65m)
Glen Finglas	56	Brig o' Turk	NN 530073	13½ miles (21.5km)	5½ hrs	1,968ft (600m)
Inversnaid and Rob Roy's Cave	18	Inversnaid, on east shore of Loch Lomond	NN 336088	2 miles (3.2km)	1½ hrs	492ft (150m)
Killin – Finlarig and Loch Tay	14	Killin	NN 574332	2 miles (3.2km)	1 hr	328ft (100m)
Lennoxtown and Campsie Glen	28	Lennoxtown, Chapel Street car park	NS 629777	5 miles (8km)	2½ hrs	686ft (209m)
Loch Ard	32	Forest Enterprise car park, Milton	NN 498010	3¼ miles (5.2km)	2 hrs	230ft (70m)
Stirling, Wallace Monument, Cambuskenneth Abbey	50	Stirling, Broad Street	NS 794936	5½ miles (8.9km)	3 hrs	364ft (111m)
Stronachlachar and Loch Arklet	36	Stronachlachar Pier	NN 404102	5 miles (8km)	3 hrs	870ft (265m)
Whangie, The	20	Queen's View, between Drymen and Milngavie	NS 511808	3 miles (4.8km)	1½ hrs	1,171ft (357m)

Comments

Beinn Dubhchraig is a Munro and this route initially takes the path towards the summit. En route it passes through remnants of the ancient Caledonian forest, keeping close to a mountain stream.

Beinn Tharsuinn and Beinn Lochain are two rarely climbed summits overlooking Loch Goil. Their ascent calls for some energy and map-reading skill, but in good conditions the scenery is your reward.

Although it is only half the height of a Munro, Ben A'an is a rewarding hill to climb. The views from the top are fabulous, and the unrelenting steepness of the path makes the walk a good test of fitness.

This varied and energetic walk takes in three glens and a series of superb viewpoints, as well as climbing to the highest point in the Ochils.

This is the highest summit of the Trossachs, an imposing mountain which features in many famous views. Although of modest height, Ben Ledi must still be respected – climb it only in good conditions.

The popular route is well-trodden and presents little difficulty. Note that in summer the start of the walk can be reached by ferry from Inverbeg, thus avoiding a long drive up the east shore of the loch.

The ascent of these two mighty peaks demands both stamina and map-reading skill. The view from the top of Ben More takes in half of Scotland and on a clear day you will see England and Ireland too.

The climb to the Ben Venue ridge from the shore of Loch Katrine calls for a fair amount of energy, but the striking views back over the Trossach mountains give an excuse for frequent rests to gain breath.

The summit provides majestic views over Loch Earn to Ben Lawers and beyond. The approach is on a clear path, but the return calls for hillcraft as it descends to a path leading to Glen Vorlich.

There is a choice of routes here and the strenuous will probably prefer to visit The Brack (2582ft/787m). The longer circuit only calls for two steepish climbs and the views are hardly less striking.

The Cobbler – the summit of Ben Arthur – has a contorted shape which has made it the best-known Trossachs mountain. Its popularity has led to path erosion and the going is quite difficult near the top.

The West Highland Way is followed through forest and moorland to Conic Hill, which rivals Ben Lomond as a viewpoint. The return from Balmaha initially follows the main road which has a wide footpath.

Soon after the start there is a gruelling climb up Grey Height, at the far end of the ridge to Cruach Ardrain. This ridge-walk to the Munro is exciting, as is the return route beside a refreshing burn.

This walk in the Ochils includes a wooded glen, an isolated reservoir and dramatic views of a medieval castle.

The climax of this short and undemanding walk is a series of waterfalls situated in a beautiful sylvan glen. It is a wonderful place to picnic on a hot day.

The Luss Hills are farmed for sheep so dogs are unwelcome. Doune Hill gives views to all points of the compass, and the walk along the ridge from Beinn Eich is immensely enjoyable.

Although Dumyat is a modest hill, the views from its slopes over Stirling and the Forth valley are superb.

This walk takes you through the beautiful wooded Strathallan, between the cathedral city of Dunblane and Bridge of Allan.

This forest trail follows part of the Highland Boundary Fault; a leaflet available from David Marshall Lodge explains local geology. The viewpoint shows all the major summits of the Southern Highlands.

This circuit of the wooded shores of Gartmorn Dam provides spectacular views of the Ochils.

This is a lengthy walk on clear tracks taking you into the heart of very wild country. Note that the tracks were made for stalking deer: in the season check that shooting is not taking place on the hill.

The West Highland Way is followed along a remote Loch Lomond shore to the famous cave supposed to have been a hideout of Rob Roy. The return climbs a path to a grand viewpoint.

A disused railway track leads to a path through lochside and riverside meadows which may become waterlogged after heavy rain. This makes a delightful evening stroll.

A walk along the track of a disused railway is followed by a short exploration of a popular glen. There are fine views of the Campsie Fells.

This is a walk for all seasons. Picturesque Loch Ard gives birth to the River Forth amidst low, wooded ridges and knolls, backed by horizons rising to Ben Lomond, the first giant of the Highlands.

The walk is packed with fine views and a great deal of historic interest – castle, abbey ruins, medieval bridge, site of a battle and a monument to a great Scottish hero.

There are great views on this undemanding walk between lochs Katrine and Arklet, culminating in a wonderful panorama of the 'Arrochar Alps'. The approach drive to the start is wonderfully scenic.

The Whangie is an impressive canyon of tumbled rocks which has long puzzled geologists. After threading through it, the path climbs Auchineden Hill, overlooking the Clyde Valley and Loch Lomond.

Introduction to Loch Lomond, Trossachs, Stirling and Clackmannan

Walking in Scotland is quite different from walking south of the border, and though the Southern Highlands may sound tame at first compared with the mountainous regions further to the north, within them are peaks that deserve every respect. In England there are only eight summits that top 3,000ft (914m), while in Scotland there are 277, with 45 of those lying within the Southern Highlands. Although this book does not embrace the mountains to the north of Glen Dochart and Loch Tay (where Ben Lawers, the monarch of the Southern Highlands, is situated), there are challenges enough in the area covered. The most demanding walk in this guide features a ridge walk involving a total ascent in excess of 5,000ft (1,500m).

Munros and Corbetts

Walkers in Scotland will inevitably become acquainted with the term 'Munro', which simply indicates one of the 277 distinct Scottish mountains whose summits top 3,000ft (914m). The name is taken from that of the 19th-century Scottish climber who first listed them, and now it is a popular pursuit for many to try to 'bag' them. Less known, and perhaps more fun, are the 'Corbetts', the summits of which lie between 2,500ft and the magic 3,000ft (762–914m). Because they are usually relatively unfrequented they present a challenge as formidable as many Munros. Altogether there are 223 Corbetts.

A secluded waterfall on the Fault Trail

Important differences

Even on the lesser walks visitors will notice important differences from walking south of the border. Most notably there is little waymarking to be seen away from the routes adopted by the Forestry Commission and a few large estates. Several of these forest and estate walks are featured in the early pages of this book. However, some of the moderately demanding routes (colour-coded blue) and most of the really challenging ones (orange) involve sections over open hillside where there are few indications of paths other than those made by sheep.

In Scotland it is difficult to devise the sort of circular footpath routes that are popular with southern walkers. The shepherd's daily walk nearly always covers different ground, and he usually heads straight up or down the hillside, either on foot or using an all-terrain vehicle. It is the sheep rather than the shepherd who make the paths, and their aims are usually not in sympathy with those of the hill walker. The ancient drovers' routes are more useful and abound in the Highlands; the herds were driven through mountain passes (*bealach* is the Gaelic word for these, and will frequently be seen on maps) either to market or to fresh pastures. New roads built for the Land Rovers of modern day stalkers often follow these traditional routes.

The Southern Highlands have always been the playground of outdoor enthusiasts from Glasgow and the other industrial and mining towns of the Clyde and Forth valleys. The building of railways brought the mountains within reach of workers who on Sundays took the trains to places like Arrochar or Crianlarich and spent the day on the hills. Walking and climbing became the recreational pursuits of many thousands of ordinary people who lived in the tenements and back-to-backs. Instead of the circular routes popular today, the walking then was most often across country from station to station and often incorporated a couple of Munros. Certainly the contrast between the flat, smoky expanse of the industrial plain and the mountainous wilderness just to the north could hardly have been greater, and the latter could be reached from many nearby urban areas within an hour.

The geology of the area

Of course, this contrast is due to geology. The line between highlands and lowlands follows that of an enormous earth movement that took place some 400 million years ago; faint echoes of this cataclysmic event are still felt here occasionally as very mild earthquakes. To the south of the fault the rock is younger and softer, being mainly sedimentary sandstones of the Devonian and Carboniferous eras. In places volcanic activity burst through these sediments and altered them, creating highland outliers such as the Campsie and Ochil hills.

The easiest way to gain an understanding of the geology of the area is to follow Walk 7 (The Fault Trail), where the Forestry Commission give storyboard explanations of the Highland Boundary Fault on the ground where the events happened. This is both an enjoyable and educational route.

Long after the formation of this fault, during the final stages of the last Ice Age (about 10,000 years ago), glaciation wrought the final geological changes. Feeder glaciers from the mountains to the north of the Forth and Clyde brought rock and gravel debris, which was added to the spoil of the enormous glacier that occupied this central rift. These glaciers smoothed and steepened the corries of the mountains in their upper parts, and chiselled out broader valleys as they descended. Later, as they melted, they dumped their debris, leaving heaps of highland rock in locations far away from where it originated. Sometimes, where there was an upstanding volcanic extrusion, the glacier left a 'crag and tail', the tail being the moraine, the material torn from mountainsides far distant and piled up behind the crag like the tail of a comet, a gentle slope descending from the top of the steep rock face that had faced the glacier.

The Trossachs, Loch Lomond, Stirling and Clackmannan
The geology means that the area covered by this book lies within the Highlands. At its heart is the small area known as the Trossachs – by rights just the richly wooded glen between lochs Katrine and Achray, but usually taken to describe a tract of country extending northwards from Aberfoyle to include lochs Ard, Katrine, Achray and Venachar. It is the district's tree-fringed lochs, rather than the hills that surround them, which give it its rare beauty and character. The name 'Trossachs' is derived from the Gaelic and means 'bristly country'. The scenery here is particularly spectacular when clothed in the colours of autumn.

Loch Lomond lies to the west of the Trossachs and shares with them the aura of romance that was bestowed on the district first by Wordsworth and Coleridge but then more famously by Sir Walter Scott, who made the Trossachs the setting for *The Lady of the Lake* and *Rob Roy*. Both areas suffer from being overwhelmed by tourists in the holiday season but comparatively few venture far from the lochside roads, and peace and beauty can readily be found in the hills, especially away from the more famous heights.

The north-eastern extremity of the area covered here is dominated by Loch Earn's Ben Vorlich. To the south west an exploration of the strange geological feature known as The Whangie gives yet another perspective of the mountains of the Southern Highlands, as well as a view over the vast plains of the Clyde and Forth.

The main town in the region is Stirling in the south east, dominated by its imposing castle and the nearby Wallace Monument. It lies near the foot of the Ochil Hills, whose rounded grassy slopes rise abruptly from the lowlands of the Forth valley. The Ochils rise to over 2,300ft (701m) and provide excellent walking, spectacular views and the chance to explore some of the delightful wooded glens that cut into their lower slopes.

Taking sensible precautions
Although much of the countryside lies at a lower level and is less forbidding than, say, that surrounding Glen Coe, nevertheless considerable heights lie within it, and none of the Munros of the Southern Highlands should be

Loch Katrine from Ben Venue

thought of as easy. Popular hills like Ben Lomond or The Cobbler are busy with walkers throughout the summer, and though these demand respect, the less frequented mountains are more dangerous simply because if accidents do happen here it is unlikely that there will be anyone nearby to give assistance or go for help.

In these Pathfinder guides the walks are graded in difficulty, beginning with the easy ones and ending with the most demanding in terms of both stamina and navigation. Make no mistake: the latter routes given here are not for the casual walker in trainers and T-shirt. They are immensely enjoyable and satisfying, but should only be undertaken in good conditions, by fit walkers who are well equipped. The times given at the start of each walk are only approximations, and adequate time must be allowed to take account of slight accidents of navigation or changes in the weather. It is no joke to be benighted and lost on the higher slopes of Ben More or Cruach Ardrain even in good conditions, and each year people lose their lives on comparatively easy hills that seem to offer few hazards.

These disasters, which often stem from seemingly trivial mishaps, are made far less likely if you take sensible equipment. Boots are essential, even though you may be able to escape with dry feet on one or two of the easier walks in a dry summer; good, comfortable boots not only keep your feet dry but also support the ankles, which can easily be turned on slippery rocks. A windproof, waterproof jacket should also be carried. Though the day may seem blisteringly hot when you set out, by the time you reach the 3000ft (914m) contour the temperature may well have dropped by more than 10°, and the wind will bring an unwelcome chill rather than the comforting coolness looked for when you were energetically climbing. On the other hand, many casualties on the tops of mountains are the result of heat exhaustion and dehydration, so be sure to have a water bottle with you and drink water rather than soft drinks, which will increase your thirst rather than assuage it. A beer hidden in a burn near the start of the walk is something to look forward to on the way down.

The food you carry up mountains should be light, refreshing and nourishing: do not take salty items like potato crisps, which by the time you get to the top will be pulverised. Sweet things also increase thirst; apples, nuts and raisins are ideal.

Take relevant maps to complement this guide (see page 95). The appropriate 1:50 000 sheet will allow you to work out where you are in relation to more distant landmarks, and a compass (essential for the more difficult walks) not only tells where you are heading but enables you to pin-point your own position and identify mountains on the

Ben Ledi from Stank Glen

horizon. Learn how to use the compass by practising when you are out on the easier routes. A whistle and first-aid kit complete the emergency gear (see the section *Safety on the Hills* on page 93).

Many walkers accustomed to the Highlands would add an anti-insect cream or ointment to this list. The midge is a curse seldom mentioned by tourist literature. It may be tiny but it is a man-eater and it particularly likes damp, misty conditions. It is unlikely to be encountered in strong sunshine or on windy days. The common fly is another plague, but unlike the midge this seems to prefer sunshine.

Due regard to local interests

Although it is difficult to miss the 'tourist routes' up popular hills such as (again) The Cobbler or Ben Lomond, be warned that the popular way of high level walking in Scotland, up to and on top of the ridges, often entails choosing your own way over rough and virtually pathless ground. The right to take one's own route at will over the open land of the hill has been important to generations of walkers and climbers in Scotland. Long an unwritten right it is now enshrined in the Land Reform (Scotland) Act 2003. These rights must however be exercised responsibly as detailed in the Scottish Outdoor Access Code to take account of the need to help land managers to work safely, to protect the environment and to respect people's privacy and peace of mind.

Deer-stalking

Deer-stalking is an emotive topic, and its main reason is often overlooked. Deer are essentially forest animals and with the destruction of their original habitat in the unregimented forests they are now having to live in hard, unnatural conditions. They often have to be fed and their numbers controlled by culling, otherwise they starve. Nobody has devised a better control system than simply shooting the weaker animals.

Unfortunately, many estates undercull, and in a wet late springtime you may well come upon the sad spectacle of dead deer. The culling of the stags, from mid-August to the end of the third week in October, is a vital part of an estate's economy, and keeps the local herd going. For this reason (and, of course, to avoid danger to themselves) at this time walkers should keep away from areas being stalked.

The hinds are culled by the keepers over the winter when there are fewer people on the hills, but the same courtesy is expected. For instance, if a Land Rover is seen at a corrie mouth it is likely that shooting is taking place, and it would be selfish of the walker to barge in and ruin a day's work. Calving time is June, and a dappled calf found on a hillside should *not* be touched. It is not abandoned, and the returning hind may reject her calf if it smells of humans.

A vast area of countryside

This book covers a vast area of countryside within which, of course, changes are taking place all the time. Large areas of forest planted over fifty years ago are now maturing and as a result considerable forest clearing and extraction is taking place throughout Scotland. This will result in temporary closure of some paths, re-routing of others and a wholesale change to large tracts of countryside. It will also provide an opportunity to see those areas as they were long before the forests came.

Above all remember that it is not obligatory to walk any route in its entirety. The approaches to many of the mountains are frequently the best parts of the walk, with the final struggle to the summit often satisfying pride more than anything else. Should you choose to descend the way you have climbed you will have the view in front of you: the further up you go, the longer this will last.

Killin – Finlarig and Loch Tay

Start	Killin
Distance	2 miles (3.2km)
Approximate time	1 hour
Parking	Municipal car park at north end of village
Refreshments	Pubs and tearooms in Killin
Ordnance Survey maps	Landranger 51 (Loch Tay & Glen Dochart) Explorer 378 (Ben Lawers & Glen Lyon)

There can be no doubt that this is the most level walk featured in these pages. It follows the line of the old railway which once ran from the village to a pier at the head of Loch Tay where passengers would disembark on to a steamer. When the loch is reached a return is made by loch–and riverside meadows to Killin, which means 'long village' – it extends for more than a mile (1.6km) north to south. This makes a relaxing evening stroll after energetic walking elsewhere, though the meadows may be wet after prolonged rain.

The old railway which once linked Killin with a steamer pier is now a public walkway and can be joined at the car park. Turn north (left) on to its trackbed and cross the iron bridge over the River Lochay. Meall Garbh is the splendid mountain dominating the landscape ahead.

Trees effectively hide the ruins of Finlarig Castle, on a hillock on the left, which was the headquarters of the Campbells in Breadalbane after they bought the Auchmore lands in the fifteenth century. A gruesome feature of the ruins is the 'beheading pit' where the Campbells disposed of prisoners they were unable to ransom. Before the Campbells came to the district this was MacNab land, and they continued to live here, somewhat uneasily, after they had finally mortgaged most of their estate to the sixth laird in 1553. The MacNabs lived in a fine house close to the castle and their relationship with their powerful neighbours was ever stormy. General Monk had to intervene to prevent violence between them during the Commonwealth.

Beyond Finlarig the track runs on an embankment parallel to a road on its left. On the right there are disused telegraph poles in the undergrowth and occasionally there are old sleepers underfoot too. Gradually the shore of the loch draws nearer; turn off the railway through a kissing-gate on the right Ⓐ to reach a lovely path which follows the edge of the loch. The shoreline is fringed by sandy beaches backed by grand trees, many of them oaks. There is a richly wooded island where the two rivers flow into Loch Tay,

The Falls of Dochart are at the entrance to Killin village

and here the path turns westwards to return to the bridge crossed earlier.

Recross the bridge and then, if time permits, turn left off the old railway B to follow another riverbank path to reach the mouth of the River Dochart. The water meadows support a grand variety of wildlife – dippers and waders will be seen in the river, while hares enjoy grazing the rich grassland.

The path soon reaches the railway again, this time by an imposing masonry bridge C (note that the five arches are concrete, one of the first examples in Britain of this material's use in such work). Turn back from the bridge along the old railway to reach the car park, deviating briefly from the track to pass through the site of the station, later used as a cattle market. ●

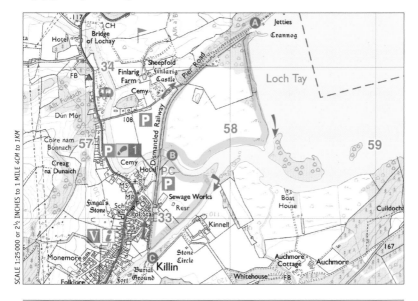

Donich Water and Lochgoilhead

Start	Lochgoilhead
Distance	2½ miles (4km)
Approximate time	1½ hours
Parking	Turn left onto Hall Road just before Lochgoilhead store. Continue along this to reach the primary school on the left and turn right into the Forestry Commission car park.
Refreshments	Pub and restaurants at Lochgoilhead
Ordnance Survey maps	Landranger 56 (Loch Lomond & Inveraray), Explorer 363 (Cowal East)

A very pleasant short walk which leads to a sylvan gem – a rock pool the size of a swimming pool, fed by waterfalls. More falls are close by, and there can be few more delightful places to picnic. Alternatively refreshment can be obtained on return to the village.

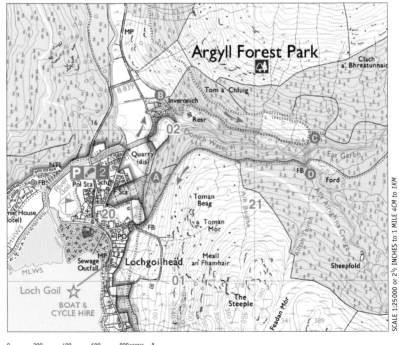

Take the path from the car park along the edge of some woodland, then turn left onto a forest road at a T-junction Ⓐ ignoring signs pointing right to forest walks. Keep on this road to reach the bridge over Donich Water then continue on the road, following red waymarker posts to reach Inveronich Farm Ⓑ. Turn right here and head round the side of the farm. In a short distance a red waymarker will indicate a path leaving the road to the left and heading uphill through woodland. Take this steep but quiet hillside track through mixed forest with occasional views to the right over the loch. The sound of the rushing stream drifts up from below as the path levels out after an initial steep climb. The hill to the right is An Stiobull (The Steeple).

Within half an hour the path twists down to the stream below, crossing the first of two bridges above a waterfall and pool Ⓒ. This bridge spans Eas Garbh, the following one Allt Airigh na Creige: the two streams join together at this point to make Donich Water. The

Lochgoilhead

waterfalls at the meeting of the two burns are at their best after a period of heavy rain and it's almost worth doing the walk in wet weather to witness this spectacle. The right of way from Glen Croe is joined just before the second footbridge. Turn right on to this Ⓓ to cross over the bridge and view another lovely rock pool which has three cataracts spilling into it.

The walk back is hardly less pleasing: it passes through shady woodland at first with the stream close by, and then emerges on to the open hill with the forest to the right. The route back from here is clearly marked by red waymarkers and has some splendid views over the village and Lochgoil to Beinn Tharsuinn and Beinn Lochain, and the hills above Lettermay which you can visit on walk 21.

Turn sharply to the right when the track meets another just before the village Ⓓ (or descend to Lochgoilhead if you seek refreshments). Turn left when you reach the junction marked by the forest walk sign and walk the short distance from here back to the car park. ●

Inversnaid and Rob Roy's Cave

Start	Inversnaid, on east shore of Loch Lomond
Distance	2 miles (3.2km)
Approximate time	1½ hours
Parking	Car park at Inversnaid pier
Refreshments	Inversnaid Hotel
Ordnance Survey maps	Landranger 56 (Loch Lomond & Inveraray), Explorer 364 (Loch Lomond North)

Rob Roy had many caves in the area covered by this book, but this is one of the best known, as it is pointed out to passengers aboard Loch Lomond pleasure steamers. This walk can be enjoyed by those using the ferry from Tarbet to Inversnaid, though the drive up the long road to Inversnaid, past Loch Chon and Loch Ard, is memorably beautiful. The route includes an enticing section of the West Highland Way, and a detour on the way back through RSPB woodland gives superb views of Loch Lomond and the surrounding hills.

Illustrated leaflets on the RSPB reserve are available at the start of the walk or from the hotel. Look at the waterfall at the south end of the car park before setting out. It is supposed to have inspired Wordsworth's lines *To a Highland Girl*. Later, Gerard Manley Hopkins also immortalised Inversnaid in verse:

What would the world be once bereft
Of wet and wilderness...

Some backpackers on the West Highland Way, passing by on a particularly moist day, might regard his sentiments with some cynicism.

🖊 Follow the West Highland Way northwards from the car park. Birch and oak trees frame views of the loch from the first, though the power station and traffic noise on the ever busy main road are intrusive. The broad, well-surfaced path narrows and is rougher underfoot after the boathouse is reached Ⓐ and two burns are crossed. Look for members of the famous Loch Lomond herd of wild goats here. In fact they are not at all shy and kept King Robert the Bruce warm when, a fugitive, he sheltered in a cave here. In better times, remembering their companionship, he passed a law allowing free grazing for these goats.

In places steep crags crowd above the path, which soon comes to a great tumble of rocks below even higher crags. Steps have been made to help walkers climb this obstacle, but care is still needed, especially if the stone is wet. More steps lead down on the far side of the massive pile of rocks, and here a sign points out a path to the left

SCALE 1:25000 or 2½ INCHES to 1 MILE 4CM to 1KM

```
0     200    400    600    800 METRES   1
                                         KILOMETRES
                                         MILES
0     200    400    600 YARDS            ½
```

painted on the rock above its entrance are for the benefit of boat passengers. The cave itself is a disappointment anyway, being just a larger cleft amongst the tumbled rocks. However, the spot is ruggedly beautiful and deserves its legacy of romance.

Unless you would like to explore further along the West Highland Way (though be warned that the going gets wetter further north) turn back along the way you have come. When you hear the rushing waters of a burn, but before reaching it, look for steps ascending on the left **C**. Take this detour (which entails quite a long climb) to explore an RSPB reserve embracing an area of woodland covering the hillside above the loch. You will see many nesting boxes in the trees; at the right time of year these may house pied flycatchers, which are becoming rare in these parts. Other birds to be seen in spring and summer include great spotted woodpeckers, various warblers and pipits, and birds of prey such as kestrels and buzzards. There are seats in two strategic positions which give wonderful views over the loch and make the strenuous climb worthwhile.

The path descends through the woods to reach the West Highland Way again close to the boathouse **A**. Turn left to pass the boathouse and return to the starting point at Inversnaid. ●

leading to Rob Roy's Cave **B**, which may well have been the one used earlier by King Robert.

Only the sure footed should attempt the scramble above the water to reach the cave. The enormous white letters

---

Loch Lomond from the RSPB path

The Whangie

Start	Queen's View, on A809 between Drymen and Milngavie
Distance	3 miles (4.8km)
Approximate time	1½ hours
Parking	Queen's View car park
Refreshments	None
Ordnance Survey maps	Landranger 64 (Glasgow) Explorer 347 (Loch Lomond South)

Opinion is divided on the nature of the geological process which caused the Whangie, a remarkable canyon reached by a short but scenically spectacular walk. Beyond the Whangie the path climbs up to a splendid viewpoint on Auchineden Hill which overlooks the Clyde Valley in one direction and Loch Lomond in the other.

There are two geological explanations for the formation of The Whangie (either glacial plucking or an earthquake), however most locals will tell you that it was actually created by a flick of the Devil's tale as he flew over here anticipating the pleasures that awaited him at the Witches' Sabbath he was about to attend at nearby Stockie Muir.

🔖 At the start there is a staircase of old wooden railway sleepers, designed

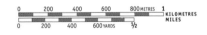

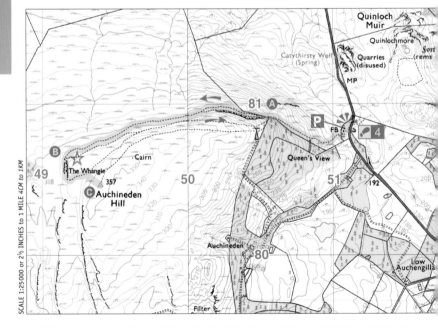

to protect the hillside from excessive erosion (the land is under the care of the National Trust for Scotland). After this, continue climbing the hill to a stile  at the top corner of the wood. Cross the stile and take the lower path keeping close to the fence. The dramatic impact of the Whangie is best experienced if, when alternatives are offered; you keep to the lower path on every occasion. This path is vague when it threads through a small boulder field below a cliff-face. Keep to the lower edge of the boulders, away from the base of the cliff. Loch Lomond can be seen in the distance. The fence swings away from here, but remains in sight.

The next rocky outcrop on the skyline is the Wee Whangie which is a sort of trailer for the real thing. None the less it provides a good scramble and squeeze for children. It is followed by another boulder field overlooked by rock pinnacles. Continue on the lowest path around the shoulder of the hill without gaining much height. Suddenly the steeples and pinnacles of the Whangie itself appear, and the path winds beneath the faces beloved by rock climbers ⓑ. Even though the heights are very modest, there are several routes which demand of the climber considerable skill and agility.

On the far side of the fissure the path climbs round the hill (note the reservoir on the right) and passes into a more conventional gorge; at the top of this

The Whangie

bear right on a distinct path which leads up to the triangulation pillar on top of Auchineden Hill ⓒ. On a clear day it is an excellent place for hill spotting: Ben Lomond can hardly be missed but many other summits will not be quite as easy to identify.

From the triangulation pillar ignore all other paths and return the way you came. Erosion from thousands of pairs of boots is destroying the terrain. By keeping to the main path you will help it return to its natural state. ●

Gartmorn Dam

Start	Gartmorn Dam Country Park
Distance	3 miles (4.8km)
Approximate time	1½ hours
Parking	Gartmorn Dam Country Park
Refreshments	Drinks at Visitor Centre
Ordnance Survey maps	Landranger 58 (Perth & Alloa), Explorer 366 (Stirling & Ochil Hills West)

This short, flat and easy walk is a straightforward circuit of Gartmorn Dam. Much of the lake shore is tree-lined, and the constantly changing views are superb, especially from the south side of the lake, looking across the water to the formidable looking line of the Ochil Hills.

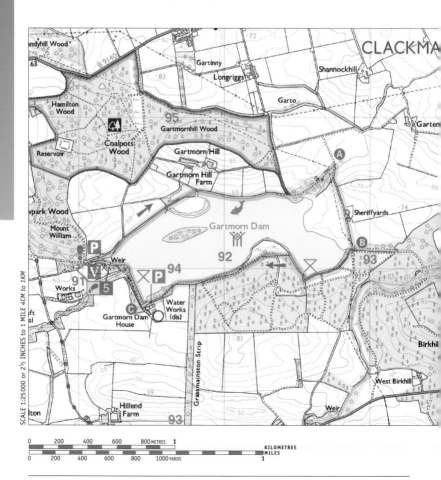

In the attractive and tranquil surroundings of Gartmorn Dam Country Park, it is difficult to believe that this was once a busy and noisy industrial area, with several coal mines in the vicinity. The dam was constructed in the early 18th century by the Earl of Alva for a dual purpose: to supply water power for the pumping engines in his coal mines and to provide water for the local population.

The walk starts by the visitor centre. Facing the water, turn left along a tarmac drive which curves right to cross an outlet burn. Immediately turn right along a tarmac drive by a car park and go through a gate at a public footpath sign. Keep ahead – there is initially a parallel footpath and cycleway – and at the next footpath sign continue beside the mainly tree-lined shores of the lake. The path later heads through woodland, passing the ruins of former colliery buildings, to a T-junction Ⓐ.

Turn right along an enclosed track which – after passing a farm – narrows to a path. After crossing a footbridge over a burn, turn right Ⓑ along a path that keeps close to or beside the curving southern shore of the lake. From this section of the walk there are magnificent views looking across the water to the line of the Ochils. Soon, after ascending and descending steps, the path reaches a T-junction Ⓒ.

Turn right onto a tarmac path that runs across the top of the dam and then curves left to return to the starting point. ●

Looking across Gartmorn Dam to the Ochils

Dumyat

Start	Parking area on lane signposted to Sheriffmuir, about 1½ miles (2.4km) north of where it leaves the A9 between Bridge of Allan and Stirling University
Distance	3 miles (4.8km)
Approximate time	2 hours
Parking	Beside lane to Sheriffmuir
Refreshments	None
Ordnance Survey maps	Explorer 366 (Stirling & Ochil Hills West), Landranger 57 (Stirling & The Trossachs)

Despite a modest height of 1,371ft (418m), Dumyat, the most westerly of the Ochil peaks, is a fine hill to climb and gives magnificent views over Stirling, the Wallace Monument and the Forth valley, plus more distant vistas of the Trossachs and Pentlands. As the starting point is fairly high up, the climb is an easy one, with just one brief steep and rocky stretch near the end, and the paths are clear throughout.

The parking area is near a pylon and a bend in the lane.

Climb the stile onto the open hillside and at a fork a few yards ahead, take the right-hand path. From this path there are superb views to the right of the buildings of Stirling University, the Wallace Monument, Stirling Castle and across the Forth valley. Follow this clear, broad path between bracken to a fork and keep ahead along the left-hand path, heading uphill.

The path curves left, continues steadily uphill and goes over a slight knoll to reach a T-junction **A**. Turn right, descend into a dip and, as you head up again, the monument on the summit of Dumyat comes into view. At a fork about 100 yds (91m) before reaching the rocky cliffs of the summit cone, take the left-hand path to a stile. Climb it, turn right along the base of the rocks, and the path curves left for the

Dumyat

final climb – steeper and rockier – to the 1,371ft (418m) summit **B**. In clear conditions the magnificent views from here extend to the Trossachs and across the Forth to the line of the Pentland Hills near Edinburgh.

Retrace your steps to the T-junction **A** and, instead of turning left, keep ahead, passing to the right of the knoll. The path then undulates across the hillside before descending to the starting point of the walk. ●

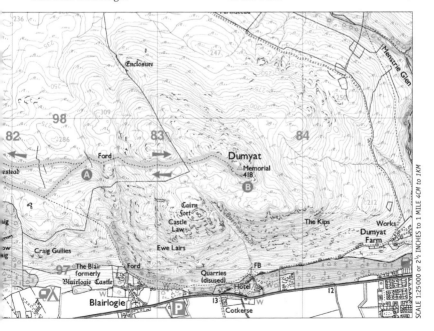

The Fault Trail

Start	David Marshall Lodge, Aberfoyle (Visitor Centre for the Queen Elizabeth Forest Park)
Distance	3 miles (4.8km)
Approximate time	2½ hours
Parking	Forestry Commission car park at David Marshall Lodge off A821 ½ mile (800m) north of Aberfoyle
Refreshments	Tearoom at David Marshall Lodge
Ordnance Survey maps	Landranger 57 (Stirling & The Trossachs), Explorer 365 (The Trossachs)

Anyone wishing to understand the geology of the area should walk this route in Achray Forest, which covers an important part of the 390-million-year-old Highland Boundary Fault. Apart from excellent scenic features (waterfalls and a superb viewpoint being the most outstanding) it is the explanatory storyboards at points of interest that give the walk its fascination. A leaflet on the Fault Trail is available from the Lodge. Paths are occasionally closed for timber felling (tel. 01877 382258).

Take the path on the left side of the Lodge, initially following the Waterfall Trail. However, this soon goes its separate way, and the Highland Boundary Fault Trail (which has

David Marshall Lodge

distinctive blue waymarks) leads over a raised timber walkway before dropping down to the stream with its 55ft (16.5m) waterfall Ⓐ. Cross the bridge below the waterfall and then turn left up a forest track (keep a sharp lookout for fast moving mountain bikers here). The

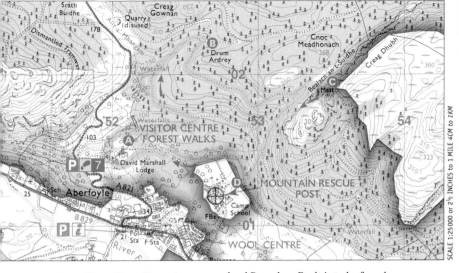

SCALE 1:25000 or 2½ INCHES to 1 MILE 4CM to 1KM

| 0 | 200 | 400 | 600 | 800 METRES | 1 |
| 0 | 200 | 400 | 600 YARDS | ½ | |

KILOMETRES
MILES

information posts on this section explain about slate and tree planting.

Bear left at the track junction and climb until, with the sound of a waterfall close by, you see a blue waymark pointing into the woods on the left. This allows a pleasant diversion from the forest track, leading down to the side of a burn. Turn right to follow this upstream to another information board, this one telling of the 'enduring dynamics of geology'. To illustrate the point there is a beautifully secluded little waterfall close by. Return to the main track and turn left to continue climbing.

At a major track junction **B** (the theme here is the ever active earth) turn sharply to the right to pass an exposure of Leny Grit, a typical rock of the Southern Highlands, being meta-morphosed sand and gravel. After this the track bends to the left and drops, before resuming its ascent; it is a considerable distance to the next information board (Volcanic Hills), where there is a seat and a fine view south to the Campsie Hills. The High-land Boundary Fault is to be found a little further on, between two boards placed close together. A nice touch here is the shape of the post bearing the information board about the Fault, the reversed Z representing the movement of the two parts of the earth's crust.

The radio mast can now be clearly seen ahead above Lime Craig Quarry, where limestone was worked until about 130 years ago. Move on to the next information board and having read its content turn left at the bottom of the quarry to climb to the hill **C** above, a wonderful viewpoint for all the major peaks of the Southern Highlands. In season there are enormous blaeberries at the top.

Return to the quarry and follow the steep, rough path down. This incline was used by the railway that took the limestone down to kilns at the bottom, where it was turned into quicklime. Both red and grey squirrels live in the deciduous woods here. Cross a forest track and turn right **D** when the path meets a second track through mixed woodland, passing above the school used for outdoor pursuits. Finally, bear left off this track on to a path leading directly back to the Lodge. ●

Lennoxtown and Campsie Glen

Start	Lennoxtown, Chapel Street car park
Distance	5 miles (8km)
Approximate time	2½ hours
Parking	Lennoxtown
Refreshments	Pubs at Lennoxtown, café at Clachan of Campsie
Ordnance Survey maps	Explorer 348 (Campsie Fells), Landranger 64 (Glasgow)

The first part of the walk mostly follows a disused railway track below the Campsie Fells to Clachan of Campsie, situated at the entrance to Campsie Glen. This is followed by a brief but highly enjoyable tour of the glen before climbing above it to a road. The return leg consists of a descent along the road and a final stretch along a path and track. There are many superb views of the Campsie Fells and across the valley of Glazert Water.

Turn right out of the car park along the road and opposite School Lane, turn left along a track. At a fork, take the left-hand path along the edge of a recreation ground and, in front of a footbridge, turn right onto a path **Ⓐ**. The next part of the walk follows a stretch of a former railway line that ran between Glasgow and Aberfoyle. In the

Alicompen Waterfall in Campsie Glen

Victorian era and later, it brought thousands of visitors to Campsie Glen.

Pass beside a barrier, go under a bridge and continue along this pleasantly tree-lined path. There are fine views of the Campsie Fells to the right, and Glazert Water is on the left. On reaching the drive to Lennox Castle Hospital, turn left and then almost immediately turn right, pass beside a barrier, cross a footbridge over a burn and turn right. At a fork, take the right-hand path **Ⓑ**, passing beside a barrier, which keeps beside the burn and at a footpath post, pass beside another barrier and turn right along a track to a road.

Turn right, take the first road on the left **Ⓒ**, signposted to Clachan of Campsie, and follow it into this delightful village of craft workshops, coffee shop and the ruins of St Machan's Church. Turn right through the village square and, at the corner of the buildings, turn left to a public footpath sign to Campsie Glen and walk along an enclosed path to a gate. Pass beside it and, at a fork immediately ahead 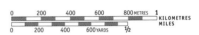, take the left-hand path through the glen for a short distance, as far as a warning notice about the danger of rock falls.

Retrace your steps to the fork and turn sharp left onto a path which winds steeply uphill, going through two kissing-gates. At a footpath sign, a brief detour along a path to the left, going through another kissing-gate and descending steps, brings you to the attractive Alicompen Waterfall. Return to the main path, turn left, and the path bends right to a car park.

Walk through the car park to a road E, turn right and follow the winding road (Crow Road) downhill for nearly 1½ miles (2.4km) to the edge of Lennoxtown. There are fine views over the valley but take care; there is not much of a verge though the road is generally quiet.

At a footpath sign to North Birbiston Road F, turn left along an enclosed path, which curves left to emerge onto the end of a track.

Turn right along the track that curves left across a recreation ground. Turn right to continue along a tarmac track, pass through gates onto a road G and turn right. The road curves left to a T-junction where you turn left to return to the starting point.

SCALE 1:25000 or 2½ INCHES to 1 MILE 4CM to 1KM

Dollar Glen and Glenquey Reservoir (vertical side text)

Dollar Glen and Glenquey Reservoir

Start	Dollar Glen, car park by old quarry, signposted from A91 at Dollar
Distance	5 miles (8km)
Approximate time	2½ hours
Parking	Dollar Glen
Refreshments	None except for seasonal tearoom at Castle Campbell
Ordnance Survey maps	Explorer 366 (Stirling & Ochil Hills West), Landranger 58 (Perth & Alloa)

Do not let such names as the Burn of Care, Burn of Sorrow and Castle Gloom (an earlier name for Castle Campbell) put you off what is a most attractive and interesting walk and anything but gloomy. A steady climb, first along the side of Dollar Glen and then through conifer woodland, is followed by a walk through a narrow valley, hemmed in by the steep slopes of the Ochils, to the lonely shores of Glenquey Reservoir. From here you return to the glen for a short but quite energetic walk through it, enjoying beautiful woodland, some impressive cascades and a series of spectacular views of Castle Campbell.

Turn right out of the car park along the tarmac track through the glen and go through a gate beside a cattle-grid. Keep ahead through a small car park and, at a public footpath sign after the next gate Ⓐ, bear right onto an uphill track that heads across the hillside.

Go through a gate to enter conifer woodland and at a three-way fork take the middle path, which continues through the tightly packed conifers to a kissing-gate Ⓑ. Go through, turn right, and the route continues through a narrow glen, between steep slopes on the left and the edge of the conifer forest on the right. After going through the next kissing-gate, keep ahead along a gently descending grassy path and, just after passing the end of the conifers, a fine view opens up ahead across open country to Glenquey Reservoir. Follow the path down to the end of it, negotiating a series of stiles

Castle Campbell

and gates and fording a small burn **C**.

From here, retrace your steps to the tarmac track **A** and turn sharp right downhill for a short circuit of Dollar Glen. On this part of the walk you enjoy a series of spectacular and photogenic views of Castle Campbell. The castle was built in the late 15th century – later extended and modernised – and, as its name indicates, was the stronghold of the powerful Campbell family, earls of Argyll.

The track curves left to a ford, where you cross a footbridge over the Burn of Care, and continues to the gates of the castle. In front of them, turn right onto a narrow path that heads down to a gate. Go through and continue descending steeply into the glen, turning sharp left down steps to cross a footbridge over the Burn of Sorrow. Cross another footbridge and follow the path up steps, continuing steeply up to pass through a fence gap at the top **D**. Here is probably the most dramatic viewpoint of all of the castle, and there is also a fine view looking down over Dollar and the Forth lowlands.

At a fork, take the right-hand path – waymarked with a white arrow – which heads quite steeply downhill along the right, inside edge of the woodland, via steps in places. Later it bends sharply to the left and zigzags down more steps, finally turning left to cross a footbridge over the burn. At a crossing of paths –

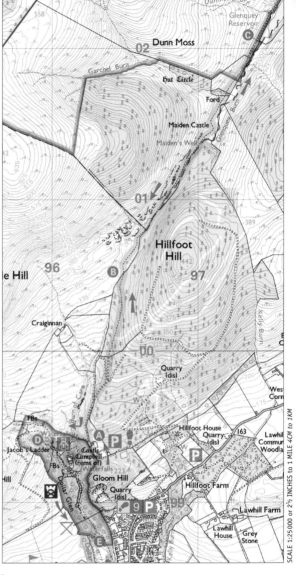

by a Dollar Glen information board – turn left **E** along a path by the burn, heading up to reach a viewpoint.

Turn right up steps, continue through the glen and, where a path comes in from the right, turn sharply onto it, initially almost doubling back. The path zigzags steeply up more steps and at the top, keep ahead through the trees and go through a kissing-gate to return to the starting point. ●

Loch Ard

Start	Milton hamlet, 1¼ miles (2km) west of Aberfoyle
Distance	3¼ miles (5.2km)
Approximate time	2 hours
Parking	Forest Enterprise car park off the B829 at Milton. Take the first turning on the left after leaving Aberfoyle then follow the signs
Refreshments	Pubs and cafés in Aberfoyle
Ordnance Survey maps	Landranger 57 (Stirling & The Trossachs) Explorer 365 (The Trossachs)

The Water of Chon and Duchray Water join together at Milton to create the River Forth, beginning its journey to Scotland's capital city and the North Sea. At the heart of the Queen Elizabeth Forest Park, the wooded knolls and ridges, clothed by Loch Ard Forest, are the first upwellings of the Highlands proper. This walk is an easy stroll along forestry roads to a peaceful lochan dappled with islets and water lilies, with a distant horizon of Ben Lomond and the crinkled hills above the eastern shore of Loch Lomond. The return stretch is along a track above the banks of Loch Ard, excellent for waterfowl and with a superb backdrop of Beinn an Fhògharaidh.

Looking across Loch Ard

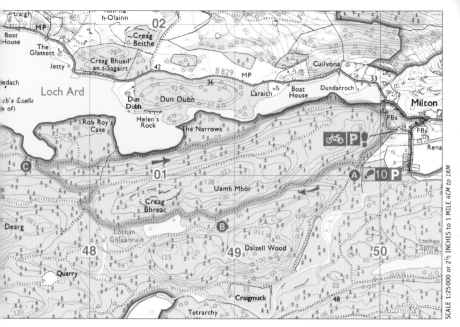

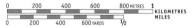

Leave the car park **A**. Ignore the turn off to the left signposted for Craigmuick Cottage and a youth campsite and keep straight ahead on a forest road. The forestry road climbs gently through conifer woods interspersed with stands of birch and moss covered oaks. Look out here in summer for pied flycatchers making the most of the wealth of insect life. The main forestry road continues to gain height easily and steadily.

In just under one mile (1.6km) again keep right at the fork **B**, shortly cresting a rise to reveal the picturesque setting of Lochan a' Ghleannain, nestling in a wide hollow beneath the bluffs of Creag Bhreac up to the right. In late summer the near end of the lochan is smothered with water lilies, contrasting with the purple hues of the heather and bright green blaeberry-clad slopes, making the most of recent forestry clearance.

Spend but a short time here and you will probably spot a buzzard or two wheeling above the ridges and various species of waterfowl – mallard, golden-eye, pochard – feeding in the margins.

Continue on past the lochan, soon reaching the highest point of the walk at a junction with a grassy forestry track to the left. Ignore this, but take the sharp right turn in a further 100 yds (91m).

This forestry road bends left to meet another; here turn left, dropping to a further junction just above the shoreline of Loch Ard **C**. Here you should turn back right, joining a wide forestry road that winds gently past several coves and inlets here at the eastern end of the loch. It is well worth dropping down to any of several gravelly beaches at the waterside to gain a fine view westwards along the loch.

From here it is simply a matter of remaining with this graded roadway. Disregard any roads or paths off to the right, eventually reaching houses on your left. Ignore the footbridge and walk round to a junction just past a gateway. Turning right here reveals the car park at the start of the circuit. ●

Ben A'an

Start	200 yds (182m) west of Trossachs Hotel
Distance	2 miles (3.2km)
Approximate time	1½ hours
Parking	Car park on south side of A821 opposite start
Refreshments	Pub, hotels and tearooms near start
Ordnance Survey maps	Landranger 57 (Stirling & The Trossachs), Explorer 365 (The Trossachs)

The view from the summit of Ben A'an is out of all proportion to the modest height of the hill (1,512ft/461m). It serves as an excellent introduction to the geography of the area, and as a test of stamina to show how fit you are before you tackle the more demanding routes which follow.

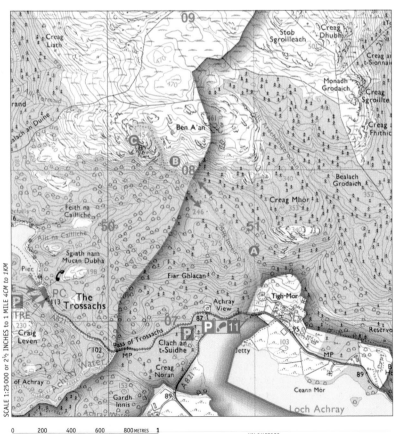

Loch Katrine from Ben A'an

Cross the road from the car park to reach a path that climbs steeply through mixed woodland and is soon accompanied by a burn on the right. The path levels out soon after crossing the burn by a footbridge A.

On the left there is a viewpoint. The path meanders through pines and when it emerges from the trees the conical summit of Ben A'an is suddenly revealed ahead. The path now becomes more demanding, a steep scramble up rock that is loosened by thousands of pairs of feet each year. Pause occasionally to catch your breath and enjoy the view looking back.

The climbers' route leaves to the left B, while the 'tourist' path continues to the top. It generally takes about an hour to reach the summit though the super-fit can do it in half this time. The highest point on the route C is 1491ft (454m) and the path ends at its twin rocky knolls each providing vistas in different directions – west over Loch Katrine and south east over Loch Achray.

Twice a day in summer the sound of a pipe band will drift up from the steamer *Sir Walter Scott* as it leaves for trips up Loch Katrine. The summit of Ben Venue looks very formidable on the other side of the water. An underground aqueduct beneath Ben A'an takes water from the Glen Finglas Reservoir to replenish Loch Katrine, which serves Glasgow and its area.

The return is by the same path and should not take much more than thirty minutes. ●

Stronachlachar and Loch Arklet

Stronachlachar and Loch Arklet

Start	Stronachlachar, on the north west shore of Loch Katrine
Distance	5 miles (8km)
Approximate time	3 hours
Parking	Stronachlachar Pier, 11 miles (17.7km) west of Aberfoyle off the B829 (park near railings to allow coaches to turn)
Refreshments	None
Ordnance Survey maps	Landranger 56 (Loch Lomond & Inveraray), Explorer 364 (Loch Lomond North)

Victorian water engineers had a field day in the Trossachs, building dams, burrowing beneath watersheds and creating subterranean aqueducts to help slake the thirst of Glasgow's burgeoning population and industries. To the north and west of Aberfoyle lochs Katrine, Arklet and Chon were laced together by underground bores in the 1850s. This walk meanders between the immense, secluded Loch Katrine and the cold waters of Loch Arklet, tracing the routes of some of these hidden watercourses amidst forests of rhododendrons and ancient birch and oak woods. A gentle climb across the watershed reveals stirring views from a modest elevation, whilst the best view is kept for the end, a stunning panorama of the 'Arrochar Alps' across hidden Loch Lomond, best seen in the morning light.

The tiny ferry terminus at Stronachlachar evokes an aura of Edwardian grandeur. Set in splendid isolation at this remote corner of Loch Katrine, the steamer *Sir Walter Scott* still calls here each midday (except Wednesdays) between Easter and October, just as she has since being launched onto the loch in 1900 when she was transported in pieces from Inversnaid (see Walk 3) by teams of horses and wagons and re-assembled in this lonely bay.

From the pier, walk back up the access road and bear left at the lodge house. Take the second roadway on the left Ⓐ, a tarred lane with a West of Scotland Water Company notice banning unauthorised vehicles, camping, bathing and fishing. This is your route for well over a mile (1.6km).

The road rises imperceptibly through stands of rhododendrons, excellent views unfolding to all points across Loch Katrine. A lively cascade on your right is the end of the underground aqueduct between Loch Arklet and Loch Katrine. Tempting footpaths branch off left, allowing access to hidden coves and

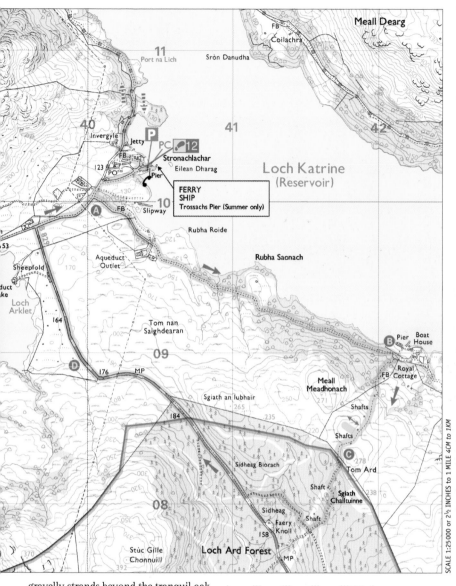

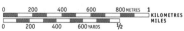

SCALE 1:25000 or 2½ INCHES to 1 MILE 4CM to 1KM

gravelly strands beyond the tranquil oak and birch woods that characterise the shoreline hereabouts. If your luck is in you may glimpse an osprey or an otter fishing the ruffled surface waters.

A cattle-grid marks the end of this road walking section. Beyond it is Royal Cottage, named for a visit by Queen Victoria in 1859 when she opened the complex of aqueducts. The way here is off to the right, up along a rough trackway ⓑ about 40 yds (36m) before

you reach the cattle-grid. This deteriorates to a well defined path through bracken and beneath trees, rising to cross a burn at a spot marked by rusty iron girders, the remains of an old footbridge. Once across take the path to the right, continuing the easy ascent and passing through an old gateway into open country. Just up

The Arrochar Alps rise beyond Loch Arklet

knoll. Walk in line beneath the power cables. It is a bit boggy in places, and the path may be smothered with deer tracks; both red deer and roe deer are common hereabouts.

The path drops to a wide forestry road. Turn right along this and follow it to the B829. Turn right and simply remain on this road. Once round the long left-hand and right-hand bends a marvellous view is revealed along the length of Loch Arklet to Ben Vorlich, Ben Vane, Beinn Ime and the other shapely summits of the 'Arrochar Alps'.

Equally eye-catching are the lower summits to the south of the loch itself, a line of craggy hills culminating in Cruachan, high above Inversnaid. How forbidding these modest hills must have appeared to the soldiers once billeted at the remote and lonely garrison (beyond the dam at the far end of the loch) during and after the Jacobite uprisings and harried by the Macgregors and the renowned Rob Roy.

At the junction, turn right to return to the pier and car park at Stronachlachar. The tiny island just off the pier once served as a prison on which Rob Roy imprisoned the factor of the Duke of Montrose until a healthy ransom was paid. It was somewhat larger until the level of the loch was raised by 17ft (5.2m) in the 1850s.

If you have time it is well worth taking the narrow lochside road north for a mile (1.6km) or so (signed through the yard of the water company complex) for some fine views up Glen Gyle and over to the crumpled peaks of Stob a' Choin. ●

from here, pass a huge pile of stones to reach a cylindrical stone tower. This is a flue from the aqueduct between Loch Katrine and Loch Chon – yes, the water is moving uphill! A line of these odd structures strides up the hillside, and this is the route to take.

Just before the third tower it is worth diverting to the right onto the hillock with a pillar near the summit. From here a great panorama of these western Trossachs opens out, with the length of Loch Katrine as the focal point, the wilderness of the Balquhidder Braes to the north, shapely Ben Venue to the east and the great bulk of Ben Lomond to the south. This is also the last glimpse of Loch Katrine until the end of the walk.

Return to the line of towers and at the next one, which is just before a hill with a pillar on top, veer right on a faint path to flank the hill and head down towards a gate in the fence. Go through this and follow the path to reach another tower. You are now in what was recently a conifer plantation but this has been felled. Follow the path to the left of the tower to skirt a

Doune Hill

Start	Glenmollochan, at head of Glen Luss
Distance	7½ miles (12.1km)
Approximate time	5 hours
Parking	Luss village car park
Refreshments	None
Ordnance Survey maps	Landranger 56 (Loch Lomond & Inveraray), Explorer 364 (Loch Lomond North)

Although Doune Hill is officially 100ft or so below being a Corbett, its ascent, with that of Beinn Eich, makes an invigorating day out. Few summits achieve such a superlative 360° view, and after the usual initial hard slog of an hour or so the going is easy. Hills like this (its top is at 2,408ft/734m) are not to be despised and climbing this one will make the walker look forward to more days on the Luss hills. This is very much a hill for sheep, and dogs are unwelcome.

There is no parking at Glenmollachan in Glen Luss and you should not park in the turning area at the farm or any of the passing places on the narrow road as this will cause traffic problems. You either have to stride the 2½ miles (4km) up the glen or bring a mountain bike and cycle up. From Glenmollachan go up the lane to Edentaggart, taking in the view up Glenmollochan at the second bridge.

🖉 After the farm (its yard can be bypassed through a sheepfold) continue up the track and pass through the gate. Here there is also a gate on the right Ⓐ which gives access to the lower slopes of Beinn Eich. Go through this and climb up with the wall to the right; as you climb note the fine corrie (Coire Cann) on the other side of Glen Luss and the view of Loch Lomond

which opens up to the east. Another gate ahead gives access to the open hill through a sheep fence. Continue to climb directly up to reach the ridge leading to the summit of Beinn Eich Ⓑ (you will find several false summits en route). The path to this first objective runs on the top of a rocky causeway (with a low cliff to the left). Ben

Loch Lomond viewed from Doune Hill

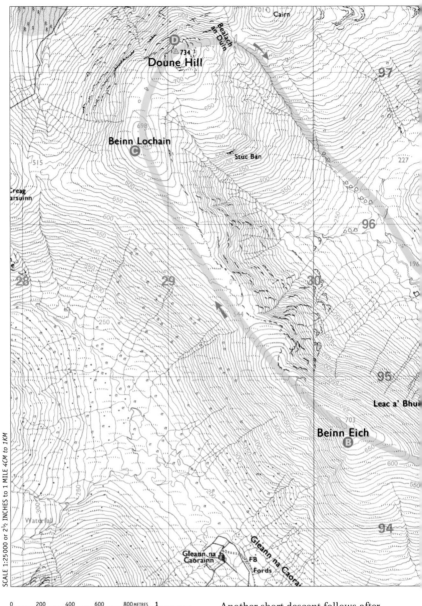

SCALE 1:25000 or 2½ INCHES to 1 MILE 4CM to 1KM

| 0 | 200 | 400 | 600 | 800 METRES | 1 KILOMETRES |
| 0 | 200 | 400 | 600 YARDS | | ½ MILES |

Lomond is well seen from here, as is the Cobbler. The summit proves to be a very narrow ridge with precipitous views down the glens on each side. The square topped hill ahead is Cruach an t-Sidhein, though the ridge bends to the right of this towards Doune Hill. Peat banks are frequent obstacles before the start of the climb up Beinn Lochain.

Another short descent follows after you reach the summit C. Now Loch Long can be seen beyond Glen Douglas, as can the summits of the Arrochar Alps. The short ascent to the tri-angulation pillar on Doune Hill D seems effortless after what has gone before. Few hills of such modest height can boast such a superb all round view.

Climb down eastwards from the summit, taking care as the ground is steep and rough in places. The unnamed

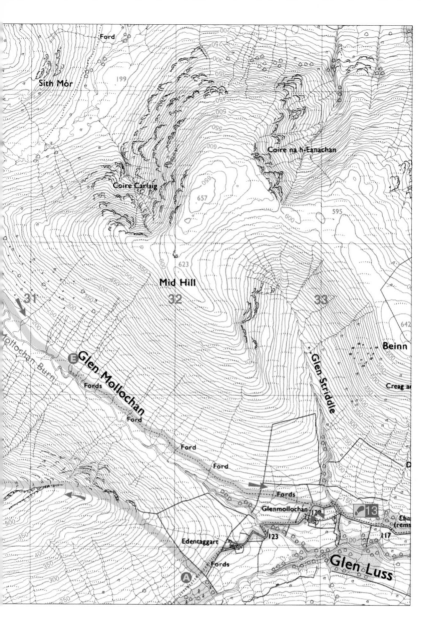

hill on the other side of Bealach an Duin looks a promising viewpoint but offers little that cannot be seen from Doune Hill. The bealach is criss-crossed by the tyre marks of shepherds' trial bikes; follow the headwaters of the Mollochan Burn down to the glen. The way down is steep and tussocky and lacks an obvious path although old fencing posts to the right of the burn may be useful as rough guides. In spring and summer a wealth of wild flowers adorn the lower

parts of the valley, amongst them several species of orchid.

At the bottom of the glen there is the vestige of a path in places but the way close to the burn is quite wet and difficult, and it is probably easiest to walk a little above the stream on the drier, north-eastern side of the glen. The Land Rover track begins (or ends) at what looks like the remains of a bothy E, and leads to the lane just above Glenmollochan, the starting point. ●

Dunblane and Bridge of Allan

Start	Dunblane, Cathedral Square
Distance	6 miles (9.7km)
Approximate time	3 hours
Parking	Dunblane
Refreshments	Pubs and cafés at Dunblane, pubs and cafés at Bridge of Allan
Ordnance Survey maps	Landranger 57 (Stirling & The Trossachs), Explorer 366 (Stirling & Ochil Hills West)

The route takes you through the attractive and well-wooded Strathallan between Dunblane and Bridge of Allan and for much of the way is either beside, above or close to Allan Water. The first half is along the Darn Road, an ancient routeway; the return takes you initially along a quiet lane before returning through woodland to the Darn Road. There are fine views looking westwards across the valley towards the Trossachs and southwards over Stirling and the Forth valley.

Start in Cathedral Square on the south side of the cathedral. Dunblane Cathedral mostly dates from the 13th century, though the oldest part, the lower part of the tower, was built in the 12th century. It has an impressive nave and fine west front. For many centuries the nave was open to the weather, following the collapse of the roof in the 16th century, but it was restored in 1893.

🖉 Facing the cathedral, turn left along a tarmac path, passing the meagre remains of the medieval bishops' palace, and the path bends right above Allan Water to the west front of the cathedral. Turn sharp left onto another tarmac path, which descends to the river, and walk along a riverside path that curves left to a road. Turn right up to a T-junction in front of the Stirling Arms Hotel, turn left and

then immediately right and head up to the main road. Cross over to a public footpath sign 'Darn Walk' and take the path through a belt of trees Ⓐ. This is the start of the Darn Road.

The path continues along the right-hand edge of a golf course to a gate. Go through and keep ahead along an enclosed path through woodland (walled in places), descending to cross a footbridge over Wharry Burn Ⓑ. At a fork just ahead, take the right-hand path, which continues by the wooded banks of Allan Water, passing a footbridge and a cave, known as Stevenson's Cave. Robert Louis Stevenson spent some time in Bridge of Allan and used to explore along the Darn Road.

The path climbs – via steps in places – above the river, then descends and bends left in front of a burn to cross a footbridge over it. Continue uphill along a wooded path, which eventually heads up onto a road on the edge of Bridge of Allan. Turn right, follow the road down to a T-junction to the left of the bridge and turn left along the main road through the town. In the Victorian era Bridge of Allan became something of a health spa, hence the hotels and large houses.

Take the first road on the left 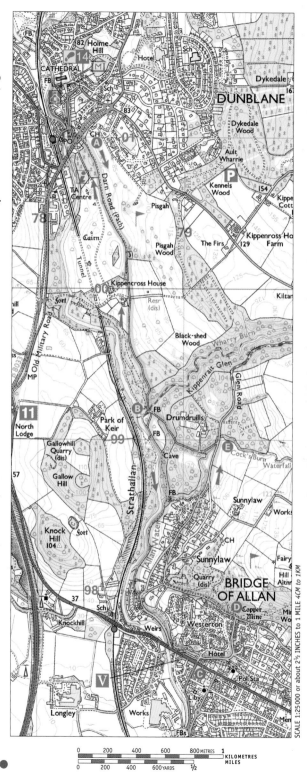, almost immediately follow the road around a right-hand bend and head uphill, curving left to a crossroads. Turn left along a road to a T-junction and turn left along a narrow road (Sunnylaw Road), which keeps along the base of steep woodland. Bear right to continue along Glen Road, at a fork take the left-hand road (still Glen Road) and follow it for nearly ³/₄ mile (1.2km) – beyond the last of the houses it becomes a narrow lane.

Look out for where you turn sharp left onto a tarmac track, crossing a burn. Where this track bends right to a house, keep ahead along a hedge-and tree-lined track that descends to a footbridge. Just before crossing it, you rejoin the outward route and retrace your steps to the starting point. ●

SCALE 1:25000 or about 2½ INCHES to 1 MILE 4CM to 1KM

| 0 | 200 | 400 | 600 | 800 METRES | 1 |
| 0 | 200 | 400 | 600 YARDS | | ½ |

KILOMETRES
MILES

The Ancient Forest below Beinn Dubhchraig

Start	Near Tyndrum
Distance	7 miles (11.2km)
Approximate time	4 hours
Parking	Look for sign to Dalrigh and Arach on south side of A82 about 1½ miles (2.4km) south east of Tyndrum. Park in large gravelled car park off the old road
Refreshments	Pub and restaurant at Tyndrum
Ordnance Survey maps	Landranger 50 (Glen Orchy & Loch Etive), Explorer 364 (Loch Lomond North)

Many approaches to the major peaks of the Southern Highlands are delightful walks in themselves. This route, which gives access to Beinn Dubhchraig, passes through a particularly beautiful remnant of the ancient Caledonian pine forest which once covered much of the Highlands. The return is made through modern plantings of conifers, a part of the walk which is far from boring since for most of the way there are splendid all round views of the hills around Strath Fillan. Note that at the forest edge on the return leg of the walk after **C** is a 6ft- (2m) high deer gate which is sometimes locked. However, the landowners have no objection to people climbing over it and this should present no problem for most walkers.

Go down the steps at the end of the car park then walk down the old road to the bridge over the river Cononish. After the bridge turn right up a track which follows the railway line westwards, crossing it about a mile (1.6km) from the river. Immediately after the bridge turn right onto a track **A** that runs beside a fence and the railway line. This is very boggy ground even in summer. Pick your way carefully to the riverbank and a bridge over the Allt Gleann Auchreoch. Turn left after the bridge following a lovely path by the burn which climbs through splendid trees, many of them Scots' pines which once formed the ancient Caledonian Forest. There are also fine birches, rowans and oaks.

The path climbs steeply around a beautiful waterfall which drops into a deep, tree-fringed pool. Cross two deer fences, about ¼ mile (400m) apart, by tall ladders. There follows an energetic ascent over open ground on a clear path – there are more waterfalls on the left and the view back is superb. Look for a solitary birch tree standing by a waterfall, cross the stream close to this point **B** and climb the slope on the

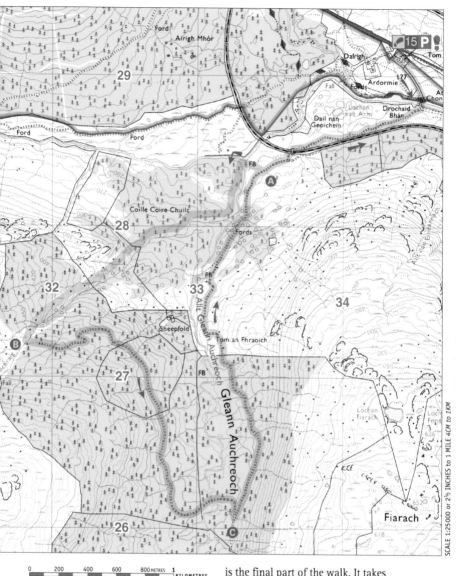

```
0        200    400    600    800 METRES   1
                                           KILOMETRES
                                           MILES
0        200    400    600 YARDS      ½
```

other side to reach the start (or end) of a forestry track.

The planting here is comparatively recent and when the trees grow they will probably hide the wonderful view, a grand panorama of the mountains to the east. Remarkably, two railways run up Strath Fillan, one on each side of the valley. On the other side of Gleann Auchreoch can be seen the track which is the final part of the walk. It takes some time to reach this – the stream must be crossed first, and then there is a short climb to reach the track heading northwards **C**.

There is more fine mountain scenery to enjoy on the final section: Beinn Odhar is the distinctive conical hill to the north of Tyndrum. The track steadily descends to reach the bridge over the railway again, and from here the outward route is simply reversed to the River Cononish and main road. ●

Ben Venue

Start	Loch Achray Hotel
Distance	6 miles (9.7km)
Approximate time	4 hours
Parking	In a layby just south of the entrance to the Loch Achray Hotel on the A821
Refreshments	Loch Achray Hotel
Ordnance Survey maps	Landranger 57 (Stirling & The Trossachs), Explorer 365 (The Trossachs)

Although Ben Venue's height (2,391ft/727m) puts it somewhat below the status of a Corbett, it demands respect as a rugged little hill, while its position overlooking lochs Katrine and Achray makes it a key viewpoint for all of the Trossachs and much of the countryside beyond. Sir Walter Scott wrote of 'huge Benvenue' in The Lady of the Lake and Rob Roy, and the exploits of the latter renegade chieftain are given some historical muscle by the fact that the Bealach nam Bo, a secret rocky defile on the flank of the hill above Loch Katrine, was used by Highlanders when they drove stolen cattle to their home glens after sorties into the lowlands. Note that the return leg of this route, through the forest, is likely to be very muddy.

From the layby walk back towards the entrance to the Loch Achray Hotel. Head up the access road then keep right to skirt the buildings before turning right to cross a bridge leading to the forest road behind the hotel. Bear right when this forks **A** (waymarked routes go to the left). Ben Venue (its name means 'mountain of the caves') looks a challenge as the track winds down through the forest with Achray Water to the right.

At the end of the forestry track climb the fence via a ladder stile **B** and continue uphill on a track running beside a fence. Ignore another stile on the right and keep on the track which will eventually join a burn to run alongside it for a short distance.

The path emerges on to open hillside giving a beautiful vista over Loch Katrine: craggy Ben A'an is clearly seen across the water, an outlier of Meall Reamhar and Meall Gainmheich. The path ends at a fence with the remains of a stile. Go through the gap where the gate used to be **C**. The route described here assaults the hill directly by following this fence up the steep north-eastern slopes; those wishing an easier alternative would continue through the Bealach nam Bo (which is facing you at this point) before swinging south to tackle the less steep northern face. In both cases paths are either very faint or non-existent.

If you decide to follow the direct route turn left and climb up with old

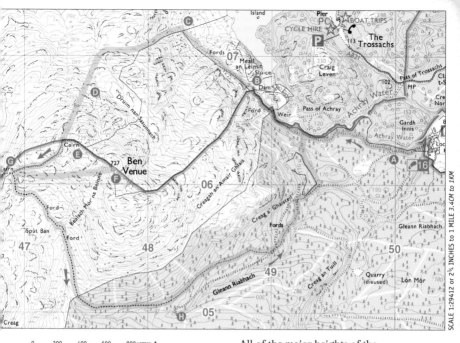

SCALE 1:29412 or 2¼ INCHES to 1 MILE 3.4CM to 1KM

fence posts to the left. There are signs of a rudimentary path through the heather and blaeberries at first, but this fades as height is gained. The slope is arduous but in recompense there are wonderful views back which will be a good excuse to catch breath. Try to keep the fence posts in sight as you climb, though owing to the nature of the ground they will tend to be further away to the left as you get higher. To the right there are impressive rocky knolls. The ascent eases as you near the top and head through a small pass to cross fairly level, if boggy, ground. Look back from here and the steamer on Loch Katrine looks like a toy and people promenading along the loch shore can only just be seen. Continue to reach a small burn. Follow the bank, crossing another burn that joins it then veer left, crossing Druim nan Sasunnach (the ridge of the Sassenach) **D** and another burn. Head for the high ground that is the ridge **E** of Ben Venue, then turn left to reach the summit **F**.

All of the major heights of the Southern Highlands can be identified from here in a wonderful panorama which extends far to the south as well. The return is made by walking back past the point **E** where the ridge was gained to reach a cairn. From here walk south-westwards to a second cairn **G** which is where the descent begins. A well-used path drops down to the forest from here, heading south. It follows the odd waymarker pole and is relatively easy to follow but inclined to be boggy, particularly in wet weather.

Cross a stile into the forest and follow a well-surfaced footpath. Continue on this as it leaves the forest then crosses a forest road **H** to continue downhill on the other side. At the junction with the next forest road turn left then, in a short distance, right beside a blue waymarker and proceed downhill on another footpath. At the next junction go left and uphill. Keep on this path to reach a T-junction with another forest road. Turn right here then left at the next junction. Keep on this road to return to the hotel. Turn left at the hotel and follow the road back to the car park. ●

Ben Ledi

Start	Corriechrombie bridge, 3 miles (4.8km) west of Callander
Distance	6 miles (9.7km)
Approximate time	3½ hours
Parking	Forestry Commission Ben Ledi car park ½ mile (800m) north of Falls of Leny car park but on western side of A84 (look for sign to Strathyre Forest Cabins)
Refreshments	Pubs and tearoom at Strathyre
Ordnance Survey maps	Landranger 57 (Stirling & The Trossachs), Explorer 365 (The Trossachs)

Although at 2,883ft (879m) Ben Ledi does not attain Munro status, it is the highest summit of the Trossachs and is visible from many places to the east. It dominates Callander, is well seen from Stirling and can even be identified from the Cheviots on an exceptionally clear day. The route described here climbs up by picturesque Stank Glen and then strikes west to reach the ridge at Bealach nan Corp. The summit lies about a mile to the south. Note that it would be unwise to attempt this route unless the weather is set fair.

🖊 Do not take the path to Ben Ledi which begins at the parking place but instead walk northwards along the track on the west bank of the River Leny – in Gaelic the *Garbh Uisge* (the old trackbed of the railway runs parallel to this on the right and this is a popular route for cyclists). After a few cottages the lane becomes a forestry track and begins to climb. Ardnandave Hill is the impressive summit which is visible ahead at this point.

Take the left fork just after the track swings away from the old railway, and at the first sharp bend in this track **Ⓐ** a footpath (marked by a white and green waymark painted on a rock) goes into the trees straight ahead. This climbs directly to another track. The path continues to the right of the hairpin bend here to reach a third track with a burn close by, which you cross **Ⓑ** to a

path opposite marked by a white post. This is steep but the walking very pleasant by the side of the stream.

The path emerges from the forest into a perfect Highland glen **Ⓒ**. The direct way to the summit is to climb up the very steep slope on the left following the edge of the trees. This is a rugged and exhausting route. The one suggested here lies more to the right (north-westwards) where the gradient is less severe and there are still waymarks (yellow ones) to guide you. The path enters the forest again briefly and climbs on the left side of a burn to reach open hillside. Turn left at a yellow and green waymark to pass through a few more trees, then follow the path up the open hillside again to reach the fence. The waymarking ends here **Ⓓ**.

Cross the stile and continue to climb

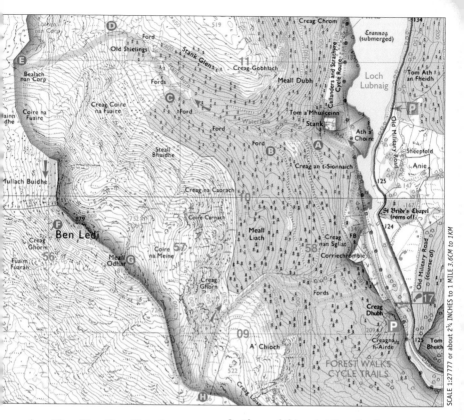

SCALE 1:27777 or about 2¾ INCHES to 1 MILE 3.6CM to 1KM

towards the ridge. This part seems endless but at last broken fence posts can be seen marking the crest. This is the Bealach nan Corp **E** which takes its name from the Lochan nan Corp a short distance to the north of this route. A funeral party from the glens to the west, travelling in winter to St Brides Chapel on the bank of the River Leny, once foolishly attempted to cross this tiny loch, but the ice broke and corpse and mourners were all lost.

The climb is still strenuous as the fence posts are followed southwards. Glen Finglas Reservoir can be seen on the right and Loch Lubnaig to the left. The final ½ mile (800m) is on top of the ridge on springy grass and makes the exertion of the ascent seem a small price to pay for the view, which is even better from the summit **F** with its triangulation pillar.

Just beyond this point there is a large cairn bearing a cross made of old fence posts. It should have taken you about two hours to reach this point.

The way down from the summit follows the conventional path, still keeping close to the old fence posts to reach the cairn on Meall Odhar **G**. Loch Venachar and the Lake of Menteith can be seen ahead. The path bends sharply to the left **H** (away from the fence posts) before meeting a Land Rover track. The forest serves as a lovely foreground to views of Loch Lubnaig.

Cross the fence into the forest and follow the well-maintained path down. Duck boarding is used to take the path over boggy areas eroded by the passing of too many boot-clad feet. Although the descent is steep the numerous burns which accompany it provide welcome refreshment as they tumble over nearby rocks. The path ends at the Ben Ledi car park at the bridge over the Leny. ●

Stirling, Wallace Monument and Cambuskenneth Abbey

Start	Stirling, Broad Street by the Mercat Cross and Tolbooth
Distance	5½ miles (8.9km)
Approximate time	3 hours
Parking	Stirling
Refreshments	Pubs and cafés at Stirling, pubs and café at Causewayhead, coffee shop at Wallace Monument, pub at Cambuskenneth
Ordnance Survey maps	Explorer 366 (Stirling & Ochil Hills West), Landranger 57 (Stirling & The Trossachs)

For such a comparatively short walk, there is a lot of scenic variety and a great deal of historic interest, much of the latter associated with Scotland's struggle for independence against England. It is part urban and part rural, partly on roads and partly on tracks and footpaths, with just one stretch of 3/4 mile (1.2km) along a busy main road. It includes a series of superb viewpoints, lovely woodland, a medieval bridge and a ruined abbey, and twice crosses the River Forth. It also passes many of Stirling's major historic buildings and if you stop to visit some of these – highly recommended – the walk will take considerably longer than three hours. There are several ascents and descents, though none of them is strenuous.

It is not difficult to see why Stirling Castle played such a vital role in the medieval warfare between Scotland and England. Occupying the top of a steep cliff overlooking the Forth valley, it both controlled the Central Lowlands and was the gateway to the Highlands. During the Middle Ages it changed hands more frequently than any other Scottish castle, until permanently retained by the Scottish kings in the 14th century.

Although there was a castle on the site earlier, the present building dates

from a programme of reconstruction carried out by successive Stuart kings during the 15th and 16th centuries, which transformed the medieval fortress into a royal palace. After James VI became James I of England in 1603 and the court moved to London, the castle was virtually abandoned, although it saw action as late as the Jacobite Rebellion of 1745.

The Old Town clusters below the castle and contains many fine buildings. Most impressive of these is the 15th-century Church of the Holy

Rude, one of Scotland's finest and largest medieval churches and scene of the coronation of the infant James VI in 1567.

The walk starts by the Tolbooth and Mercat Cross near the bottom end of Broad Street. Walk up Broad Street to a T-junction, turn left and at a footpath sign to Cowane's Hospital and Back Walk, turn right along a tarmac path that passes to the left of the Church of the Holy Rood. Do not go up the steps into the churchyard but turn left at the far corner of the 17th-century Cowane's Hospital and follow the path around a right-hand bend to descend to a T-junction Ⓐ. To the left is a stretch of Stirling's town walls.

The route continues to the right towards the castle along Back Walk, a tarmac path that follows the line of the walls. About 10 yds (9m) before a T-junction, follow the path to the left – not sharp left down steps but initially keeping at the same level – and the wooded path descends and continues below the castle walls. There are superb views to the left over the Forth valley. The path later curves right and emerges, via a kissing-gate, onto a road at a bend.

Cross over, keep ahead along a track and, at a fork, take the left-hand, lower path. Follow it across rough ground, climbing quite steeply to the cannons and Beheading Stone on Gowanhill Ⓑ, a grim reminder that this was once the scene of public executions. This is another superb viewpoint, looking across the town to the prominent

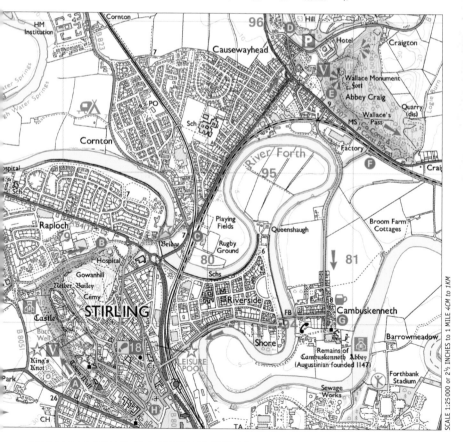

The Auld Brig, Wallace Monument and Dumyat

landmark of the Wallace Monument, backed by the line of the Ochils. From here take the steeply descending grassy path to the right of the cannons and, at a T-junction, turn left along a track that bends right to a road.

Turn left, take the first road on the right and, where it ends, keep ahead along a tarmac path that passes under the busy A84. Turn right towards the 15th-century Old Stirling Bridge and cross it. It was in the meadows near this crossing of the Forth that William Wallace gained his greatest victory over a much larger English army in 1297. Bear right through a wall gap, walk along a tarmac path to a road and take the second road on the left **C**, passing under a railway bridge. Now follows about ³⁄₄ mile (1.2km) of walking beside a busy main road to a crossroads and traffic island at Causewayhead. Keep ahead, and the road curves left to a T-junction **D**. Turn right along Hillfoots Road and, just after passing the Sword Hotel, turn right into the Wallace Monument car park.

Walk through the car park, bending right, pass to the right of the ticket kiosk and, at a T-junction, turn left onto a tarmac path, which winds quite steeply uphill through woodland to the monument on top of Abbey Craig **E**. This impressive Gothic tower, opened in 1869 as a monument to the great Scottish patriot, overlooks the scene of his greatest triumph over the English army of Edward I. There is an outstanding view looking across to the town and castle.

Retrace your steps down the tarmac path for about 50 yds (46m) and bear right, by an information board, onto a narrow path through the trees. Follow this path along the top of Abbey Craig, enjoying more spectacular views over Stirling and the Forth valley, before descending steadily through the woodland. At a fork, take the right-hand path that bends sharply right and descends to a road.

Turn right, take the first road on the left **F**, go over a level crossing and, where the road bends left, keep ahead along a tarmac track to a road. Turn left beside the River Forth and follow the road for just over ¹⁄₂ mile (800m) into the small village of Cambuskenneth. Of the Augustinian abbey founded by David I in 1147 little is left apart from the restored detached bell tower. King James III and his wife are buried here.

In the village, turn right along South Street **G** and cross a footbridge over the river. Keep ahead along Abbey Street into Stirling, following signs to Town Centre and keeping by another short stretch of the river – the Forth does an amazing series of meanders in the vicinity of Stirling. After crossing a bridge over both railway and road, keep ahead at a crossroads along Maxwell Place, bear left in front of the post office and immediately turn right up Friars Street. At a T-junction, turn right up Baker Street **H**, bear right near the top and turn left into Broad Street back to the starting point. ●

Conic Hill and Balmaha

Start	Where West Highland Way crosses the Drymen–Gartmore road
Distance	9½ miles (15.3km)
Approximate time	4½ hours
Parking	Forestry Commission car park on Drymen – Gartmore road 1½ miles (2.4km) north of Drymen
Refreshments	Pub and tearoom at Balmaha
Ordnance Survey maps	Landrangers 56 (Loch Lomond & Inveraray) and 57 (Stirling & The Trossachs), Explorer 347 (Loch Lomond South)

Prospective long-distance walkers can get a flavour of the West Highland Way from this route, which passes through forest and across open moorland before climbing steeply around the flank of Conic Hill (1,174ft/358m), a magnificent viewpoint at the southern end of Loch Lomond. Balmaha is always busy with visitors in summer, and walkers enjoying a well earned pint at the pub may well be serenaded by a piper. A direct return is made along the main road as far as Milton (there is a wide footpath) before a farm track leads off back to the forest. There is a 'No dogs' notice at the point where the Way leaves the forest for the open hill.

Take the track into the forest; this is an early part of the West Highland Way. Initially there are views towards Loch Lomond but these are soon blocked off by trees. It is easy walking on a good track. Do not take the alternative route to the left offered by a waymark after about two miles (3.2km) Ⓐ but carry straight on along the West Highland Way. The track becomes more tortuous and is lined by bluebells ('hyacinths' in Scotland, where 'bluebell' means the English harebell) and primroses in late spring. The forest road ends and the Way becomes a metalled path which leads through a camp site dedicated to backpackers. At the end of the forest there are high steps over the deer fence Ⓑ. Excellent walking follows over open moorland. The path ahead can be clearly seen climbing the eastern flank of Conic Hill. Beinn Bhreac is the greater height to the right. The path drops down to cross two sparkling burns, the first being a lovely spot to picnic, with the cool water soothing hot feet. It will be just as well to take advantage of this, as the hardest part of the walk follows.

This is the steep climb up the twisting path on the northern side of Conic Hill, which lies directly on the course of the Highland Boundary Fault (see Walk 7). It is some consolation to know that the ascent in the other direction is even steeper. Pause occasionally to enjoy the view. Ben Lomond is slowly revealed ahead, and then, as the ascent eases, Loch Lomond too comes into view. This is one of the best places for an overall view of the loch. An even wider view can be obtained from the summit of the hill, which is easily reached by paths leaving to the left. Beware of being startled here by the sudden whoosh of a passing hang-glider: they may occasionally provide photographers with unusual foreground interest in this grandest of panoramas.

The path descends steeply through Bealach Ard **C**. Deep steps make the way down awkward but safe. The path threads through a resinous pine wood with ancient Scots' pines at the top. Turn right when the path meets with a forest track **D**; in spring look to the right to view great expanses of bluebells (hyacinths!) before the track reaches the car park at Balmaha.

On warm days many walkers take the opportunity to bathe in the loch here, but alternative refreshment is available in the pub just to the right (west) of the car park.

Turn left along the main road to resume the walk. There is a wide foot-path alongside the busy road and this is followed for about an hour into the tidy village of Milton of Buchanan. Here there is a white church, village hall, school and cottages. Cross the bridge to

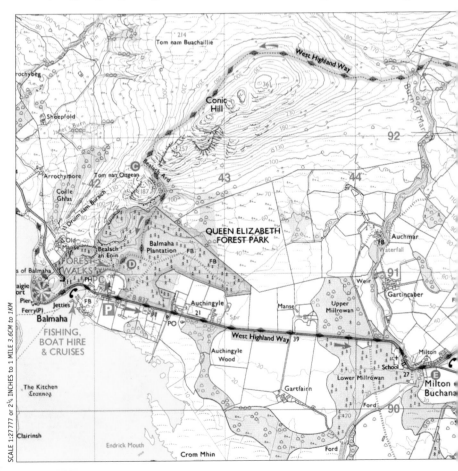

the telephone box where the route turns to the left **E** to follow a sandy track uphill. This passes the handsome farmhouse of Creityhall on the left and then continues to climb to reach the forest. There are more views to Loch Lomond on the left.

When the track joins with the West Highland Way again **A** (at the waymark mentioned earlier denoting an alternative route) turn right to retrace steps through the forest to the starting point. ●

Loch Lomond from Conic Hill

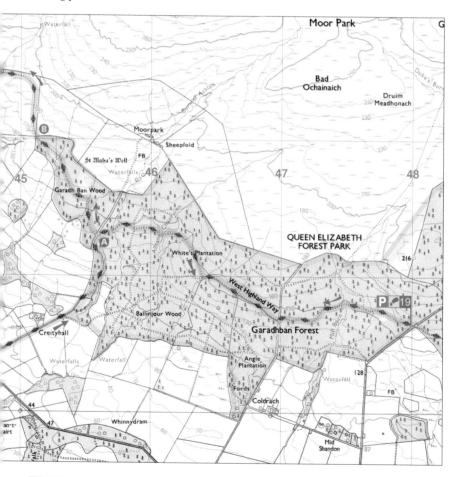

Glen Finglas

Start	Brig o' Turk
Distance	13½ miles (21.5km)
Approximate time	5½ hours
Parking	Turn off A821 into village and drive past school to where road forks and there are hydro notices forbidding further vehicular access. There is space for off-road parking here
Refreshments	Pub and restaurant at Brig o'Turk
Ordnance Survey maps	Landranger 57 (Stirling & The Trossachs), Explorer 365 (The Trossachs)

This long walk passes through the wild upper reaches of Glen Finglas, climbing to the 2,000ft (600m) contour before beginning a return leg down the equally unfrequented Gleann nam Meann. There is a good track all the way, and it would be quite hard to get lost even in poor visibility if this is followed. The circuit is a favourite with off-road cyclists who, though they will hardly catch walkers on the way up, may surprise them as they speed down. Look for stags on the skyline as you walk below the crags of Coire Ceothach and Carn Dubh. To check on access during the stalking season telephone 01877 376256.

From the end of the public road take the right fork, following the public footpath sign ('Balquhidder 10 miles'). The road climbs up steeply, accompanied by the sound of rushing water from the left. Soon the concrete dam can be seen through the trees, and after half an hour's walking the track emerges into open country and there is a splendid view of the Glen Finglas Reservoir as well as a sobering one of the track winding up into the mountains far beyond its head. As you walk up beside the reservoir beyond the farm (where the surfaced road ends) the route to be followed looks even more daunting. In a year of drought when the water in the reservoir is low the small island at its southern end resembles the

top of a coconut. Ben Ledi is well seen to the right.

After about an hour the track divides **A**, a mile (1.6km) or so from the head of the reservoir. Keep to the track following its shore, crossing the bridge over Allt Gleann nam Meann. Tom an Fhaile, with its crown of trees, is no longer an island after a succession of dry years.

At the top of the reservoir the track descends steeply – a brief respite before a long, unrelenting climb. There are plenty of trees in the glen at first but gradually these thin out as height is gained. Soon the reservoir is hidden

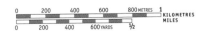

Glen Finglas

epfold

Ban

Mainnir Feidh

Creag na Croiteige

Tom a' Phearsain

Ford

11

Creag na h-Airighe

FB

Cladh nan Casan
Waterfall

A

Sròn Achaic na h-Airde

51

52

Tom an Fhaile

53

10

Lagnan nan Searrach

Meall Gainmheich
566

Coill' Dhuingeanna

Creag na h-Airigh

Geal Chreagan

Glen Finglas Reservoir

09

Ford

Sheepfold

Stob Sgroilleach

Creag Dhubh

Tom a' Ghille Mhuirich

Tom Buidhe

Creag an t-Sionnaich

Monadh Grodaich

Creag Sgroilte

Creag an Fhithich

Glen Finglas

Ard Achadh

Tom Earraich
226

Toman Dubh

Creag a' Bhlàir

en A'an
461

Bealach Grodaich

352

Creag Mhòr
353

246

Sròn Armailte
367

08

Dam

Power Station

Glen Finglas Road

Tom nan Gaothaizean

Weir

Sgiath Mhic Griogair

20

Ghlacan

Achray View

Tigh Mòr

87

P

P

95

103

Reservoir

Cnoc nan Sidheag

07

Tom na Caillliche

123

Sch

Cemy

Jetty

MP

89

Blair House

Ceann Mòr

92

Feadan a Bhlair Choig

Brig o' Turk

MP 86

Brig o'Turk

Inn

Bad Biorach

821

Loch Achray

Achray Farm

SCALE 1:25000 or 2½ INCHES to 1 MILE 4CM to 1KM

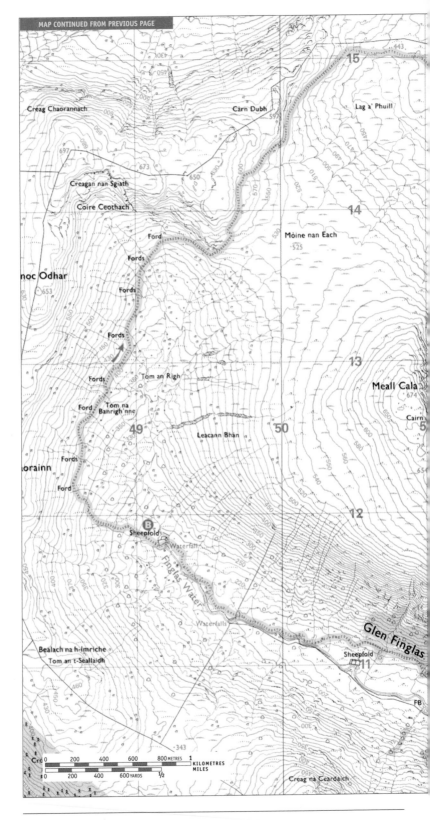

15

Creag Chaorannach

Càrn Dubh

Lag a' Phuill

697

673

650

Creagan nan Sgiath

Coire Ceothach

14

Ford

Fords

Mòine nan Each

·525

noc Odhar

653

Fords

Fords

13

Meall Cala

674

Fords

Tom an Righ

Cairn

5

Fords

Tòm na
Banrigh'nne

49

50

Leacann Bhàn

65

orainn

Fords

Ford

12

B

Sheepfold

Waterfall

Finglas Water

Waterfalls

Glen Finglas

Bealach na h-Imriche

Tom an t-Seallaidh

Sheepfold

11

FB

·343

Cro

| 0 | 200 | 400 | 600 | 800 METRES | 1 |
KILOMETRES
MILES

0   200   400   600 YARDS   ½

Creag na Ceardaich

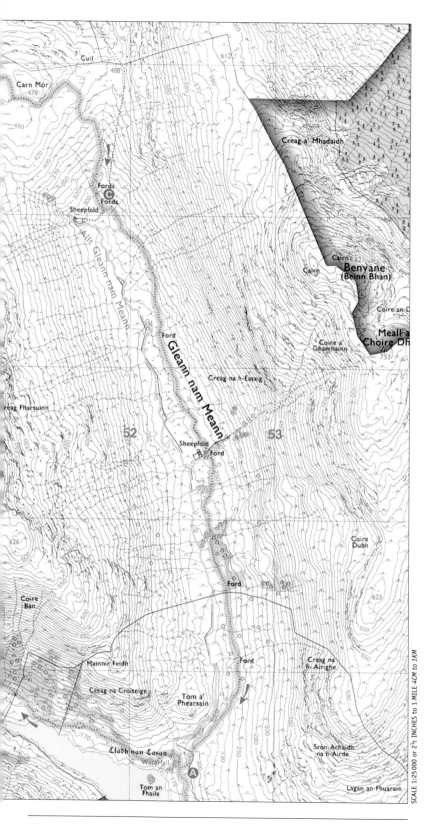

SCALE 1:25 000 or 2½ INCHES to 1 MILE 4CM to 1KM

from view, though Ben Ledi still overlooks the glen.

After approximately three hours' walking (after a ford and sheepfold) Ⓑ the track leaves Finglas Water and begins to climb more seriously (in compensation the reservoir is in view again to the south east, and the track can be clearly seen ahead climbing up the flank of the hill towards the sky-line). Small birch trees manage to survive here, almost at the top of the glen. Deer on the crest of the hills above the track look down without interest on walkers struggling towards the col between the two glens. Even at this height there are many refreshing burns.

The head of the pass is at last reached beyond Carn Dubh, and Benvane can be seen ahead as the track swings eastwards. A little further and Gleann nam Meann is revealed with the track clearly visible below, running south-wards. The footpath from Balquhidder joins with the track at a ford by a sheepfold Ⓒ.

At the next sheepfold down the glen a rowan tree is growing from the walls of an abandoned shieling. Soon after-wards the reservoir is in view again below, and the track descends steadily, following the stream, to reach the original track Ⓐ which follows the shore. Turn left onto this for the final part of the long walk, which will take about an hour, retracing steps along the track by the reservoir and then past the dam to reach Brig o'Turk. ●

Red deer stag

Beinn Tharsuinn and Beinn Lochain

Start	Lettermay, Lochgoilhead
Distance	7 miles (11.3km)
Approximate time	5½ hours
Parking	Limited off-road parking at Lettermay
Refreshments	Pubs and restaurants at Lochgoilhead
Ordnance Survey maps	Explorer 363 (Cowal East), Landranger 56 (Loch Lomond & Inveraray)

There is an energetic start to this lovely route around the hills overlooking Lochgoilhead. A stiff climb of about 1,400ft (400m) takes walkers above tree level onto the ridge that culminates in Beinn Lochain (2,306ft/703m), a craggy summit that is a superlative viewpoint, not only towards Loch Goil but also northwards to Loch Fyne and the mountains beyond. The descent demands care but passes by a beautiful, remote mountain loch and a spectacular waterfall. There is a burn to ford, and the going underfoot is boggy and tricky in places. Do not attempt this walk at least four days after heavy or prolonged rain as the burn at Ⓖ will be impassable, and there is no alternative route.

Take the road from Lochgoilhead, sign-posted for Carrick Castle, and park on the roadside beyond the chalet complex, at the bridge over Lettermay Burn.

🖉 If the water in the burn is at all peaty and discoloured, or shows strong flow, then *do not* start the walk. If you see low water, however, then walk a few paces back towards the chalet park and turn left up the driveway to Corrow Trekking Centre. Walk through the yard, go through the gate at the end, and then turn right to begin the demanding climb up to and through a wide firebreak which gives access to the hilltop above the trees. If you started the walk in the morning and the sun is shining, the view back will be truly dazzling. After

about thirty minutes of stiff climbing the worst is over and the tree line below.

Turn left before the rocky outcrops ahead (Creag Loisgte) Ⓐ and follow the contours above the forest, keeping high enough to allow views over the tree-tops. It would be as well to have a short right leg on this long traverse! Climb to the top of the ridge on the right Ⓑ before coming to the end of the trees for a wonderful panorama. Ben Lomond dominates the view eastwards. Continue heading north west, towards the col between Stob na Boine Druim-fhinn and Beinn Tharsuinn (this is marked as 'Coirein Rathaid', *coirein* being a diminutive form of *coire*). Although mainly pathless, the way up to Beinn

Tharsuinn is very obvious, sweeping round to approach the summit from the north east direction, avoiding a host of hillocks and outcrops. The long summit ridge holds several lochans. It will take a good two hours to reach this point **C**.

Having spent time enjoying the grand view and identifying the various summits leave Beinn Tharsuinn on the gentle south-western slope and then swing south to approach Beinn Lochain which at 2,287ft (703m) is 249ft (82m) higher than Beinn Tharsuinn. Keep as close to the edge as you dare for the best views (but be careful, for the drop is precipitous and there are many rocky outcrops to skirt). Beinn Lochain has a modest cairn at its summit **D**, which seems rather insulting for such a wonderful viewpoint. The Curra Lochain nestles below the steepling crags of Beinn Bheula, whose slopes are newly afforested, while to the west Strachur can be seen with Loch Fyne beyond. A succession of grand peaks forms the background of the vista in this direction. To the east and nearer at hand the various summits of the Arrochar Alps are more easily identifiable, particularly the distinctive shape of the Cobbler.

The recommended way off Beinn Lochain is to head west until the gradients and outcrops of the ground to the south ease to allow a safe descent. This will mean descending to the top (western) end of the lochan. The more adventurous may try a more direct descent to its lower end, but there are many cliffs and gullies hidden from above so this may prove risky.

Turn left **E** to head eastwards along the rather boggy shore of the remote lochan. At the lower end of the loch cross the Sruth Bàn (burn) and keep it on your left to reach the head of cascades **F**. Bear right (south) a

Lochgoilhead from the Sruth Bàn cascade

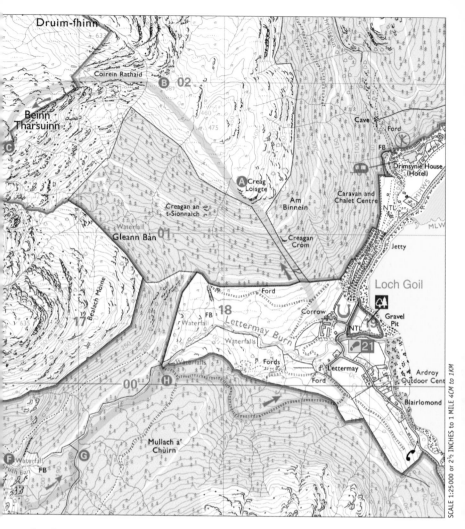

few dozen paces and then follow the faint path as it loops eastwards over a series of grassy rock bands down towards the young conifer plantation. Look for the narrow fire break that takes the path beneath the trees to emerge beside Lettermay Burn at an old stile and white post (if you cannot spot the path, simply forge a route down-slope and leftish through the trees along a planting ditch to reach the burn). Cross the fence and walk downstream through trees to the confluence **G**.

Cross Lettermey Burn here (either wading, or the nimble-footed can leap the three boulders) to pick up the path alongside the east bank of Lettermay Burn. This little valley has a wealth of bird life. Ahead are the lower flanks of Stob na Boine and the distant cone of Ben Dornich.

At the red brick gauge house at the head of some falls **H** turn back right, tracing the wide forest track up to the nearby forestry road. Turn left along this, following it down to and beyond the woodland edge. Keep left at the new bungalow to wind with the roadway past new housing and down to the tarred lane above Lettermay Bridge. Bear left to return to the start. ●

Ben Vorlich (Loch Earn)

Start	Ardvorlich, on south side of Loch Earn
Distance	7 miles (11.3km)
Approximate time	5½ hours
Parking	Off-road parking on lochside
Refreshments	None
Ordnance Survey maps	Landrangers 51 (Loch Tay & Glen Dochart) and 57 (Stirling & The Trossachs), Explorers 365 (The Trossachs) and 368 (Crieff, Comrie & Glen Artney)

Usually Stuc a' Chroin is 'bagged' at the same time as Ben Vorlich, which is logical if the main aim is climbing Munros. A well worn path from the summit of Ben Vorlich leads to that of its junior neighbour, and the adventurous could then descend Stuc a' Chroin's south east ridge to reach the ruined shieling at Dubh Choirein, which is on the footpath leading to Bealach Gliogarsnaich. However, after wet weather there may be difficulty in fording Allt an Dubh Choirein. The route described here leaves Stuc a' Chroin to the more energetic, leading off the summit of Ben Vorlich by the southeastern ridge to descend over rough ground to the path by Allt a' Bhealaich Gliogarsnaiche. At times this is difficult to follow, especially after the bealach which leads into Glen Vorlich. However, there should be no great navigational difficulties in following the burn downstream and the scenery is grand. To check on access during the stalking season telephone 01764 685260.

Hill walkers use the east driveway at Ardvorlich by the lochside bridge, walking upstream with the Ardvorlich Burn on the right at first. Note that dogs have to be on leads here. Bear right to cross the stream before the farm and then turn left immediately to start climbing up a good track on the west side of the burn.

This is a very pleasant way to climb a hill, following a good clear track up through typical Highland woods. The track forks **A** after a wooden bridge: bear right towards Ben Vorlich.

Cross Allt a' Choire Bhuidhe by another plank bridge **B** and continue to climb directly towards the handsome shape of Ben Vorlich with the stream now below to the right. The path climbs steadily up the flank of the hill's northern ridge. The view from here opens up well behind with Ben Lawers the commanding summit beyond Loch Earn; at 3,982ft (1,214m) this is the highest mountain of the Southern

Highlands. Nearer the summit the going becomes harder as the path zigzags up very steeply. However, the triangulation pillar soon comes into sight and the reward is a staggering view as befits a mountain of 3,231ft (985m). The summit is a level plateau with the tri-angulation pillar at the north-western end and a large cairn Ⓒ to the south east, about 100 yards (90m) away.

Walk past the cairn to begin the descent down Vorlich's south-eastern ridge, following a line of old fence posts. When these end, and the path becomes more sketchy, keep following the ridge down until the slope to the left becomes easy enough to allow a descent due east to the Allt a' Bhealaich Gliogarsnaiche Ⓓ (do not leave the ridge too early though, as the outcrops of Cas Dhubh are precipitous).

The path from Callander follows this stream northwards into the craggy pass between Ben Vorlich and Beinn Domhnuill – Bealach Gliogarsnaich Ⓔ. Watch for deep and dangerous potholes

The path up to Ben Vorlich

as the faint path climbs up below steepling crags. At best these will fill your boots with water; at worst they will sprain or break an ankle. Note how close the two streams are to 'capturing' each other. The steep and craggy east face of Ben Vorlich is well seen from this point.

From the head of the pass the path is very rudimentary, being more suited for sheep than humans, and following the eastern side of the Ardvorlich Burn which has a series of refreshing cataracts as it flows over rocky ledges. The view ahead is always a delight.

After a lengthy descent the path, such as it is, becomes a track when it meets the remains of a wall Ⓕ below Sgiath a' Phiobaire which is at the tree line. The track crosses the Allt a' Choire Bhuidhe close to where it joins its waters with those of the Ardvorlich Burn. This is a delightful part of the walk, the way shaded by birch and rowan trees and the stream chuckling close by. The track joins with the one used for the outward journey about a mile (1.6km) above Ardvorlich House.

The Brack

Start	Walkers' car park at Ardgartan Tourist Information Centre just off the A83
Distance	9½ miles (15.3km). Alternative version 7½ miles (12.1km)
Approximate time	5 hours (6 hours for the alternative version)
Parking	At end of public road before Coillessan Houses
Refreshments	None
Ordnance Survey maps	Landranger 56 (Loch Lomond & Inveraray), Explorer 364 (Loch Lomond North)

This is an interesting route which apart from twice climbing over the col which separates The Brack from Ben Donich has little in the way of testing gradients, unless you take the option offered here of climbing to the summit of The Brack itself (2,582ft, 787m). There are good views of Rest and be Thankful, The Cobbler and Loch Long on both routes.

Turn off the A83 to Ardgarten TIC. Go past the main car park to cross a bridge then turn right to reach the walkers' and cyclists' car park. Leave the car park and take the forest road heading north west and parked as the Cat Craig Loop, cycle path.

This road heads gently uphill and in a little under a mile turn right at a T-junction **(A)**. In a further 50 feet you will pass a white marker post for the hill access post to Brack summit. Ignore this and continue along the forest road with a view ahead along Glen Croe. General Caulfield's military road, built in the years immediately following the Battle of Culloden can be seen snaking up the Glen to the Rest and be Thankful with the more modern A82 running along the side of the Glen above it.

Keep an eye open for a white pole by the side of the road and opposite it a green sign pointing the way to the hill path to Lochgoilhead **(B)**. This is about

1.8 miles from the start of the walk. Turn left onto the path and head uphill keeping on the path until you climb a stile and reach open hillside. From here dogs must be on leads.

Follow the line of white poles uphill to the Bealach Dubh-lic, the saddle between The Brack (on the left) and Ben Donich (on the right). Pause just before you reach the top of the hill and enjoy the view back; three heights on the far side of the Glen Croe are easily identified: Beinn Luibhean, Beinn Ime and Ben Arthur, the last better known as The Cobbler.

Continue to the top of the hill, veer left to pick up the next marker pole **(C)**. The glen ahead looks bleak and the forest ahead about a mile (1.5 km) distant is the next objective unless one has the energy and the inclination to climb The Brack – a favourite height with rock climbers who can tackle routes such as Elephant Gully, the Great

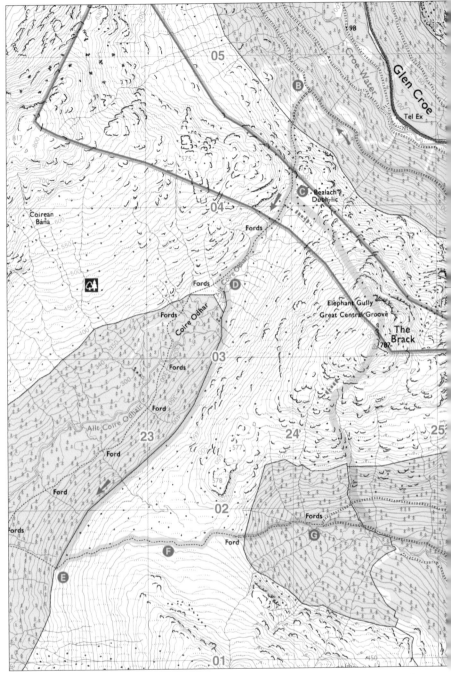

On the main route follow the line of white poles along the glen to the wood. The way is boggy but fairly easy walking. When you reach the last marker pole before the wood **D** veer left towards the corner and go through a gap in the fence (alternatively if this

Central Groove (conquered only in 1958), the Mammoth and the Big Game Route. Most of them are classed as 'difficult' or 'severe' climbs.

The view from The Brack

then, almost immediately, cross a small burn. Keep following the edge of the wood and in a short while you will reach a wide firebreak **E**. Turn left here and follow a line of white marker poles uphill. It is a strenuous climb following them to the col between Brack and Cnoc Coinnich. There are very steep cliffs on the south side of The Brack. Pleasant, more level, walking follows along the col **F** with splendid views. Glen Douglas can be seen over on the other side of Loch Long.

has been repaired, climb over it). Follow the edge of the wood to reach the next fence then climb over it and turn right.

To follow an alternative route over the Brack, proceed as follows. Descend to the white post at the bottom of the bealach and then climb directly up the opposing slope, keeping close to the burn. Near the top, traverse to the left to skirt Elephant Gully and the Great Central Groove and reach the summit.

From here go south-south-west, with the summit of Cnoc Coinnich straight ahead at this stage, to find a small burn which threads its way through rocky ground. The going is rough and requires care, especially where the stream drops down through steep gullies (traverse left to avoid the worst of these). Cross a fence and then follow down the edge of the forest, close to the stream. There is a splendid, refreshing waterfall about halfway down before the path meets a forest track. Cross this and continue down for a short distance to meet with another track, where you turn left on to the longer route.

Continue following the edge of the wood as you head uphill. This is rough, often boggy ground and the going can be heavy. Eventually you will reach another fence which you have to climb

Continue following the white marker poles across the col to reach a cairn at the other side. Descend from here to reach a stile into the woods and continue downhill on a steep but well-surfaced footpath. If you are facing a breeze you will see smoke-like mist to the right where spray is blown back from a waterfall. The path follows the right side of the Coilessan Glen steeply down through the forest. A couple of bridges **G** will carry you across the burn at the bottom and the path continues to reach a forest road **H**. Turn left and continue downhill. There are good views on this descent as there has been a lot of timber harvesting. When the road forks go right again then cross the Coilessan Burn by a bridge. Ignore the right turn here and keep straight ahead. At the next junction go left and continue until you reach a narrow, metalled, lane. Keep on this, passing the turning to Cat Craig Road. From here it is a little under two miles along this road to return to the car park. ●

The Cobbler

Start	Head of Loch Long
Distance	7 miles (11.3km)
Approximate time	6 hours
Parking	Laybys on A83 at head of Loch Long
Refreshments	Pubs and tearooms at Arrochar
Ordnance Survey maps	Landranger 56 (Loch Lomond & Inveraray), Explorer 364 (Loch Lomond North)

The alpine-like shape of The Cobbler with the fantastic overhang of its north summit can be seen from dozens of viewpoints in the region. As soon as railways provided easy access the Cobbler (it is seldom known by its alternative name of Ben Arthur) was adopted by Glaswegians as a favourite excursion, and the peak has attracted walkers and rock climbers ever since, even though at 2,900ft (884m) it does not quite achieve Munro status.

At the head of Loch Long there are lay-bys on both sides of the A83 that provide convenient (and ever popular) parking places for this walk.

🖊 A clear path enters into the trees by the Argyll Forest Park signboard and passes a cairn-like collecting box for the Arrochar Mountain Rescue team. A steep, eroded path climbs straight up the hillside through the trees, following a line of concrete blocks. When the path emerges onto a forest track, cross straight over this to continue the ascent alongside the blocks, which were the sleepers of a railway which was built to help with the construction of the Loch Sloy Hydro Scheme.

This is a hard slog to gain height quickly; a much more pleasant stretch follows when the steep path meets another running along the flank of the hillside **A**. Turn left here. Note the gleaming particles of quartz in the glistening schist, and enjoy the views over Loch Long.

After about 20 minutes' enjoyable walking on this path you arrive at a small dam **B** penning back the waters of the Allt a' Bhalachain, and the outline of The Cobbler is suddenly revealed in all its glory. This is a popular spot to rest for a minute or two before continuing to climb – the burn tumbles down over a series of small waterfalls, and the water is cool on feet which are probably already beginning to suffer.

The next part of the route is delightful. The path follows the burn on its course from the mountain. The gradient is easy and the scenery superb, with the dramatic outline of the Cobbler becoming more dominant as the mountain is approached.

The two great boulders which are passed on the way up are the Narnain Boulders: rock climbers find good practice on these, even though the pitches are short. The path crosses the burn **C** and bears away from the Coire

SCALE 1:25000 or 2½ INCHES to 1 MILE 4CM to 1KM

a' Bhalachain, soon becoming very steep as the climb up to the summits begins. There is much loose rock (which is even more treacherous in wet conditions) and the popularity of the mountain means the path is becoming very eroded. The final few metres up to the ridge are a good scramble.

From here the view is all-embracing. Ben Lomond is, as ever, an unmistakable landmark. To the north Beinn Ime blocks the view, though the main road can be seen below its flanks climbing Rest and be Thankful.

Turn to the right along the ridge to climb to the North Peak: of the three peaks this is the only one which – in spite of its incredible nose-like overhangs – is easily accessible to walkers. The infamous central peak (strictly speaking, the name Cobbler refers specifically to this rock) lies in the other direction **D**. Although it is a short and easy climb to reach the base of the rock, getting to the top is another matter and

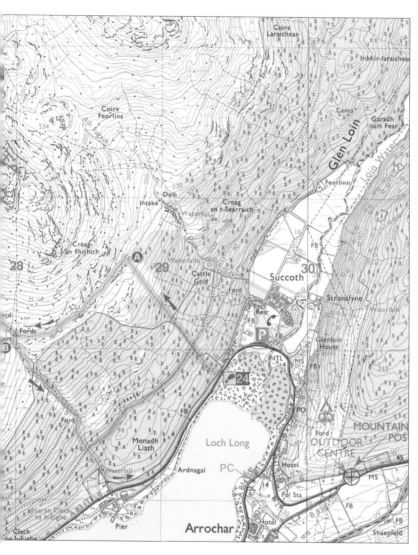

it is easy to understand why it was made a test of nerve for prospective Campbell chiefs. It entails a scramble up its bare sloping ledges to a rock window, which gives access to another narrow ledge with a drop of hundreds of feet below. This has to be traversed to the left before another brief scramble involving two easy handholds takes you to the flat roof of the summit. As with many such climbs, the way up is easier than the way down.

It is foolish to attempt to come off this mountain by the steep and eroded path used to climb it. Instead, as you return from the central peak walking towards the North Peak look for a distinct path which leaves from near the point where the ridge was reached, and heads north west. Although this becomes quite steep lower down, it is a straightforward descent leading to the Lochan a' Chlaidheimh, which is almost completely dried out now though its perimeter remains boggy. Turn to the right to reach this Ⓔ and then follow the left bank of the burn, which soon joins with the main path near the

Narnain Boulders. Continue on this down to the dam ⒷＢ.

Cross over the stream here and take the path down to the forest, turning to enjoy a last view of the Cobbler before the mountain is obscured by trees – the fantastic overhang is well seen from this point. The path down follows a raised bank with the stream on the left. When the path divides for the first time be sure to bear to the right – the other way is really rugged! There are occasional views of Loch Long below. The stream is never far away and can often be seen dashing over cataracts where there are impressive swirlpools, formed by the erosive force of the stream's waters over countless hundreds of years.

The path down continues though the views are lost once a forestry track is crossed (turn left onto this and follow it to the edge of the forest and the path by the concrete blocks if you prefer to avoid walking by the main road). Towards the bottom there is a fine waterfall where a rock spout makes it possible to actually walk behind the cascading water.

Turn left when the main road is reached and walk back to the starting point at the head of the loch. ●

The Cobbler's central peak

Cruach Ardrain

Start	Glen Falloch, 2 miles (3.2km) south west of Crianlarich
Distance	7½ miles (12.1km)
Approximate time	6 hours
Parking	Layby on south side of A82 opposite Keilator Farm
Refreshments	Tearoom and pubs at Crianlarich
Ordnance Survey maps	Landrangers 50 (Glen Orchy & Loch Etive) and 56 (Loch Lomond & Inveraray), Explorer 364 (Loch Lomond North)

At 3,428ft (1,046m) Cruach Ardrain is a formidable Munro whatever the approach. This route tackles it from the north west and after the demanding initial climb of Grey Height follows a grand ridge walk before the final steep ascent of Cruach Ardrain itself. Instead of the usual long return over Stob Garbh and Stob Coire Bhuidhe (which involves a steep and hazardous descent northwards from Cruach Ardrain) this route takes an easy way down to return along the delightful River Falloch. To check on access during the stalking season telephone 01301 704229.

Take the track which leaves at the north end of the layby, twisting down through the meadow to a sheep creep below the railway line and a bridge over the River Falloch. The Land Rover track heads into the glen overlooked by Sròn Gharbh and Meall Dhamh. At the end of the forestry plantings fork left Ⓐ on a track which drops to a bridge across the river. Cross the bridge and begin climbing up the western flank of Grey Height (why a Sassenach name for this hill?) with the forest fence to the left.

The rough grassy slope is taxing but views open up as height is gained. Crianlarich can be seen beyond the forest and, on the other side of Glen Falloch, the twin peaks of Ben Oss and Beinn Dubhchraig. The top of Grey Height Ⓑ is rocky and the ridge path bypasses the summit as it continues to climb, passing to the east of Meall Dhamh up to the unnamed summit Ⓒ which overlooks

River Falloch and Cruach Ardrain

this outlier. There is a lochan just before the top is reached. The massive shape of Cruach Ardrain looks very forbidding ahead as the path threads its way along a ledge with a precipitous drop to Coire Ardrain to the left.

The path drops down steeply to a boggy col where there are stepping stones across a lochan 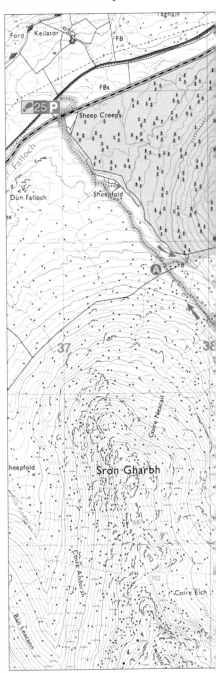. Then the steep and direct climb to the summit of Cruach Ardrain begins. As you climb there are views southwards down the narrow Ishag Glen below Stob Glas.

Cruach Ardrain (its name means 'high stack' – perhaps of peat) has a long summit ridge with three cairns, the north-easternmost of these being the summit proper ⓔ, from which there is a very steep descent to the bealach before Stob Garbh (not attempted on this route, however). The view from each of the cairns is spectacular, with an inviting range of summits seemingly linked to Cruach Ardrain by radiating ridges. This impression is deceptive, though a good path to the south gives a pleasant walk to Beinn Tulaichean – an optional extra if you have enough time and energy.

However, the recommended way is to return westwards (from the western cairn) to the col between Meall Dhamh and Cruach Ardrain. Keep a sharp lookout for a cairn ⓕ on the right of the path just before the lochan on the bealach. This cairn marks the point at which an easy descent can be made into Coire Earb. You will be heading westwards down grassy slopes towards the darkly spectacular Coire Eich on the other side of the glen, with its silvery threads of cataracts falling to the River Falloch. Small burns springing from the east side of the glen are a welcome source of refreshment after the parched summit ridge.

The craggy outcrops of Meall Dhamh ('hill of the stag') rear above as the bottom of Coire Earb is approached.

Sròn Gharbh looks a challenging top on the other side of the glen. On the eastern side there is a lone tree: pass close to this on the descent. The Land Rover track can be seen in the far distance. There are many summer flowers on the lower hillside and by the banks of the burn (the infant River Falloch). A crossing point **G** should be found before the stream grows, and the faint and often boggy path on the western side eventually leads to a sheepfold **H** which is the terminus of the Land Rover track returning down the glen to the main road.

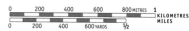

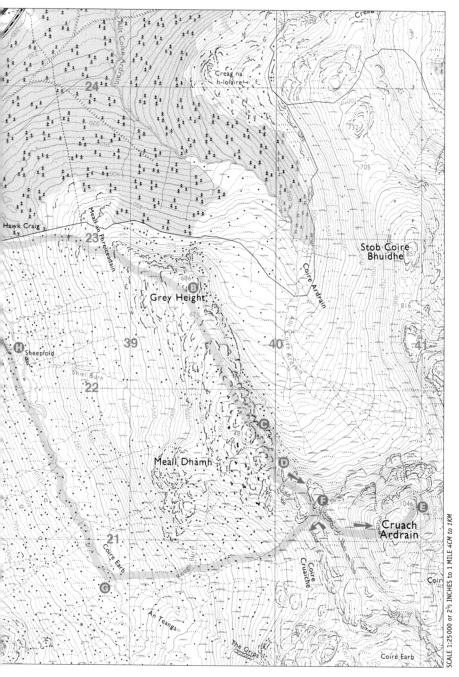

Ben Lomond from Rowardennan

Start	Rowardennan
Distance	7½ miles (12.1km)
Approximate time	5 hours
Parking	Car park at Rowardennan Pier
Refreshments	Hotel at Rowardennan
Ordnance Survey maps	Landranger 56 (Loch Lomond & Inveraray), Explorer 364 (Loch Lomond North)

If you spend any time in the area you will find yourself – like generations before you – almost inevitably drawn towards Ben Lomond and its ascent. Its name is thought to derive from an old word (Ilumnan) meaning 'beacon' and is very apposite as it is seen from all around, which also means that on a clear day the views from its summit are extensive in all directions.

The main route to the summit is that from Rowardennan; on a fine day in summer it is little more than a strenuous uphill walk on a well-established path (and mountain runners make the ascent and descent in just over an hour!). In winter, however, it can become a serious expedition when snow and ice make an ice axe and crampons necessary equipment, and at all times of the year strong winds and a marked temperature drop may be experienced as the summit is approached. Rowardennan itself is at the end of an unclassified road which often becomes congested with traffic, but the long (albeit attractive) drive from the west side of Loch Lomond can be avoided in summer by using the ferry crossing from Inverbeg.

From the car park take the path directly behind the public toilets which is signed 'Ben Lomond Path'; in about 150 yds (140m) join a path coming up from the right and continue up a wide ride (i.e. a gap between the forestry planting) between larch trees on the right and predominantly sitka spruce on the left. The gradient varies as one ascends through the forest, but the path is well constructed with a bridge over a small burn and rock steps in a steep section. There are occasional views to the left across Loch Lomond to the hills beyond, and also up to the summit of Ben Lomond and the secondary peak of Ptarmigan to its left. After ¾ mile (1.2km) a gate Ⓐ is reached at the top of the forest.

You are now passing onto land that is owned by the National Trust for Scotland; this is used for sheep grazing, and dogs must be kept on a lead. Grazing has a considerable effect on the vegetation – note the contrasting regenerated woodland in Coire Corrach to the left where sheep have been excluded by fencing. The Ben Lomond footpath is used by many thousands of walkers every year and work is undertaken to repair and improve it: foundations have been provided made of matting or rock, and some of the gradients eased by zigzagging, but most significantly drainage has been provided to reduce the erosion by water of loose material which is continually exposed by the pounding of many pairs of walking boots.

If you pause to look back, perhaps at the gate in the next fence B, you will see Inverbeg on the other side of the loch, with the sizeable delta at the mouth of Douglas Water and the wild Luss hills rising beyond. The many islands (Inches) of Loch Lomond are seen in its wider southern part. The Highland Boundary Fault runs through

The view from the summit of Ben Lomond

the largest of these, Inchmurrin, and then Creinch, Torrinch and Inch-cailloch; this is the fault line that separates the northern older rocks of the Highlands – remnants of the great Caledonian Mountain Chain – from the much younger rocks of the Central Valley of Scotland (see Walk 7).

As you continue upwards onto Sròn Aonaich **C** views of the Trossachs open up to the right with Loch Ard and Ben Venue identifiable. From here the gradient eases for a while and the path is marked by cairns which, while common in mountain areas of England and Wales, are comparatively rare in Scotland, where the hill walker is expected to be able to find the way without such aids! Across Loch Lomond to the west-north-west the craggy profile of the Cobbler, amongst the Arrochar Alps, becomes increasingly visible as you ascend.

It remains to tackle the steep final section of the ascent to reach the point on the path **D** where it attains the ridge running east-south-east from the summit, and where the views of the mountains to the north across Loch Katrine suddenly appear – a visual reward for the uphill toil! The path continues well below the crest of the ridge and rises fairly easily now to gain the summit of the Ben **E** at 3,194ft (974m). From here the Highland mountains seem to rise endlessly to the north and west, contrasting with the views south to the Central Valley and even to the hills of the Borders, the Clyde estuary with a glimpse of some enticing islands beyond to the south west, and lower hills such as the Campsies to the south east.

The descent is mainly by the same route, but those with sure feet and a head for heights can follow the crest of the ridge to point **D**, looking over the crags down into Coire a' Bhathaich. As you continue downwards on the main path the views in front and to each side can now be appreciated without the need to stop and turn round.

A further alternative route, for the final part of the descent through the forest, is available for those who would appreciate some variety. Pass through the gate at point **A** and carefully estimate 260 yds (240m) along the path from here, perhaps counting your paces. This should bring you to a point where, beneath the conifers, a path descends through the trees on the right; it is not at all obvious at the start and you may have to peer underneath the trees to see it, but you may also find a notch on a tree at the point where you turn down, which will confirm identification of the path. It quickly becomes more evident as you proceed, swinging first right and then left to emerge above a valley with the sound of a waterfall getting ever nearer. The path continues along a terrace, with the valley on the right, and views of the waterfall open up behind. Proceed through the woods with a last glimpse of the river, Ardess Burn, as it tumbles through a small gorge, and a little further on you will see a brick tank to your right. Keep to the left here; follow the path which goes on to pass between an earth bank (left) and a ruined fence (right). About 380 yds (350m) after the tank the path passes beneath an overhead power line and bears left to ascend a short way before crossing over a small burn. The final section leads downhill through some beautiful ancient oakwoods (declared a Forest Nature Reserve in 1989) with an incised valley to the left of the path, and reaches a gravel road **G** about ¼ mile (400m) north of the car park from which you started.

Ben Cleuch

Start	Alva Glen, signposted from A91 at Alva
Distance	7½ miles (12.1km)
Approximate time	5 hours
Parking	Alva Glen
Refreshments	Pub at the bottom of Mill Glen on the edge of Tillicoultry, café and restaurant at The Farriers 🕑
Ordnance Survey maps	Explorer 366 (Stirling & Ochil Hills West), Landranger 58 (Perth & Alloa)

After an initial steep ascent out of Alva Glen, the climb to the 2,366ft (721m) summit of Ben Cleuch is a mainly steady one, apart from two steep but relatively short stretches that come after leaving the track through Silver Glen. The descent over The Law and down into Mill Glen is more difficult; long and steep, with a particularly steep drop just before the end. Then follows a delightful walk through the wooded glen and the final part of the route is along a gently ascending track, partly through woodland, along the lower slopes of the Ochil Hills. There is plenty of variety and outstanding views all the way, both over the Ochils and across the lowlands of the Forth valley at the foot of the hills, but it is quite an energetic and strenuous walk. It should not be attempted in bad weather, especially misty conditions, unless experienced in walking in such conditions and able to navigate by using a compass.

Alva Glen is one of a series of thickly wooded ravines that cut into the steep southern slopes of the Ochils. The burns that flow through these glens were harnessed for water power and the 'hillfoot towns' – the settlements at the foot of the Ochils (Menstrie, Alva, Tillicoultry and Dollar) – became major centres of the textile industry during the Industrial Revolution.

🖉 Start by turning left, in front of the 'Welcome to Alva Glen' information board along the path through the glen. After bending right to cross a foot-bridge over Alva Burn, climb steps to a

T-junction, turn left and head up more steps to reach an impressive waterfall. Turn right along a path, ascend steps to a T-junction, turn left up more steps and, at the top, turn right to pass under a water pipe. Keep ahead to a T-junction and turn left. The path bends right and heads up to a gate, where you leave the wooded glen.

Bear left and climb steeply across the open hillside – later by a wire fence on the right – to reach a track Ⓐ. Turn left and follow this winding track steadily uphill, going round several bends and continuing along the edge of Silver

View from above Mill Glen

Glen, to a gate. Go through, continue up the glen above Silver Burn on the right. Later the track bends first right and then left to keep above a burn on the left.

At a gate, do not go through but turn right Ⓑ steeply uphill alongside a wire fence on the left, later levelling out to reach a stile at a fence corner. Climb it, continue steeply uphill again by a fence on the left, but later following a discernible path that veers right away from the fence and heads more gently up to the pile of stones, triangulation

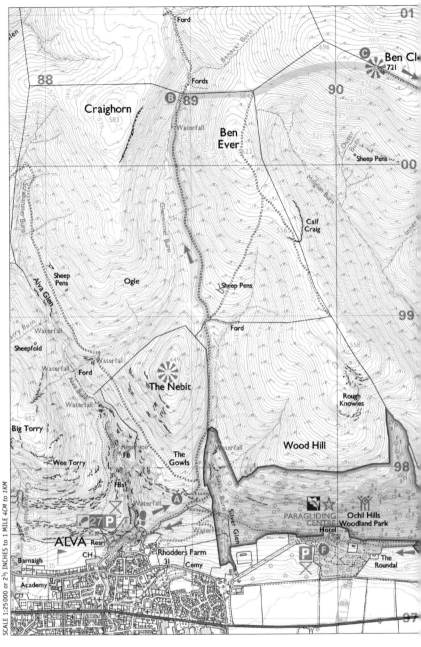

pillar and view indicator at the summit of Ben Cleuch **C**. At 2,366ft (721m), this magnificent all round viewpoint takes in the Trossachs, Pentlands and, in clear conditions, extends to the Grampians in Aberdeenshire and along the Lothian coast.

At the fence just beyond the tri-angulation pillar, turn right and keep

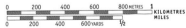

alongside it, heading downhill. By a fence corner, the path bends right, heads down into a dip and then climbs to the summit of a conical hill called The Law, at 2,093ft (638m), which affords another superb viewpoint,

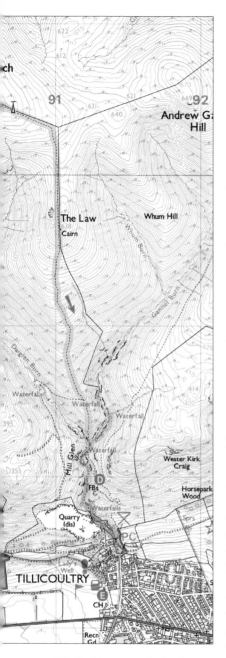

After crossing the footbridge, turn right onto a path that climbs above the burn and at a fork – by the end of a fence – take the right-hand, lower path through the glen. Now follows a most beautiful part of the walk as the path goes up and down steps, crosses and recrosses Mill Glen Burn several times and passes a number of cascades. After going through a gate, the route continues along the left-hand edge of a quarry and crosses the burn once more to emerge onto a road on the edge of Tillicoultry.

Keep ahead, passing a mill on the right. At a footpath sign, turn right over the first footbridge and keep ahead along Scotland Place. Where the road ends, continue along a track to a T-junction, turn left and turn first right along a tarmac track **E**.

Where this track bears right, bear left at a public footpath sign to Alva, along an enclosed path that runs along the right-hand edge of a golf course. The path gently ascends to enter woodland and continues first through it, then along its left-hand edge and then through the trees again to join a track.

Keep ahead – the track becomes a tarmac one – to pass The Farriers **F**, the early 19th-century stable block of the vanished Alva House, which now houses a hotel, restaurant, craft shops and coffee shop. By the Ochil Hills Woodland Park car park on the left, bear right onto a path that climbs steadily through woodland to cross a footbridge over Silver Burn. Keep ahead to go through a kissing-gate and continue along a path to a track.

Turn right and follow the track around a left-hand bend, heading up-hill. Immediately after going through a gate, turn left **A** onto a path heading steeply downhill across a field. Here you rejoin the outward route and retrace your steps to the start. •

especially looking across the Forth lowlands.

Continue downhill by the fence on the left but, where it bends left, keep ahead across the grassy slopes, heading steeply down – a lengthy and tiring descent – towards Mill Glen. Take particular care on the final difficult drop to a footbridge **D**.

Ben More and Stob Binnein

Start	Glen Dochart
Distance	10 miles (16.1km)
Approximate time	8 hours
Parking	In layby on A85 just to west of bridge over Allt Coire Chaorach, about 5 miles (8km) east of Crianlarich
Refreshments	None
Ordnance Survey maps	Landranger 51 (Loch Tay & Glen Dochart), Explorer 364 (Loch Lomond North)

This route demands both stamina and some skill in navigation. It is not so much a walk as a challenge, entailing an ascent of 4,900ft (1,500m) in total, and covering a distance of ten miles (16km), much of it over steep, rough, trackless ground. Bear in mind that if you are on the hill at 9am it may well be two in the afternoon before you reach the first of the summits. The views from the tops are stunning (said to encompass half of Scotland) and for this reason alone it is worth saving a good day for the expedition. To attempt it in poor visibility would be asking for disaster. To check on access during the stalking season telephone 01567 820487.

From the layby walk across the bridge to a gate on the right. This gives access to a track leading through a meadow (once the site of Rob Roy's house) to a green gate into the forest. The track through the forest is very gloomy but lightens when it comes to a ford Ⓐ, where it is difficult to keep dry feet even in times of drought. Stepping stones and overhanging branches are helpful. In fact there is a hazard of wet feet throughout this approach, with the path suffering from the passage of many pairs of boots.

After crossing the ford turn left along the west bank of Allt Coire Chaorach. Another sparkling burn is crossed in a refreshing glade – at this point the path is some way from the major stream, though it soon swings back to the south east towards it. However, the path emerges from the forest Ⓑ with the stream some distance to the east. It takes about an hour to reach this point. The elegant Stob Binnein and less gainly, more massive, Ben More are revealed standing majestically above the vast corrie; the route runs round the rim of this enormous basin.

Bear left across the valley over broken ground, and cross the stream and deer fence near sheep pens before attacking the climb up to the north-eastern arm of the ridge. This is the start of an unrelenting struggle up virtually pathless slopes. The first minor summit,

Leacann Riabhach, is a teaser with a succession of false summits while Stob Creagach , which follows, also has its share of these. However, it is not necessary to follow the crest of the ridge, and energy will be saved by choosing a route which does not have too many descents.

Ben More from Strath Fillan

From Stob Creagach the mountain wilderness to the east is revealed. The route drops slightly to the Bealach na Frithe before the stiff climb up to Meall na Dige – the first 3,000-footer though not a Munro in its own right. Keen-eyed walkers will find traces of a path along the ridge which drops abruptly down to a lochan **D**, the prelude to a demanding climb to Stob Coire an Lochain, the first stage of the ascent of Stob Binnein ('anvil peak').

Keep the remains of a wall to the left as you climb the ridge, taking time to draw breath and admire the views, which are magnificent here but even better from the top cairn. A lovely lochan just below the summit gives this height **E** its name, and the Stob Binnein path (now very distinct) passes the left side of this peak, dropping to a narrow col before climbing steeply to the next summit.

The only thing that mars the conquering of Stob Binnein is the prospect of the ascent of Ben More, which looks steep and forbidding from here, though this is actually deceptive. The last part of the climb up the Stob is very exciting, the best part of the route. Ben More appears much more shapely from Stob Binnein and serves as an impressive foreground for views to the north. From here the path is quite distinct, though steep and rocky, and the 1,000ft (300m) final climb up to the major summit from Bealach-eadar-dha Bheinn **F** should take only 30 minutes or so if all is going well. Crianlarich comes into view as height is gained, and from the summit **G** it is easy to believe the claim that in ideal conditions the panorama takes in half of Scotland, from Edinburgh to the islands off the west coast (as well as the north coast of Ireland – Ben More is easily identified from the Giant's Causeway), and from Galloway to the

SCALE 1:27777 or about 2¼ INCHES to 1 MILE 3.6CM to 1KM

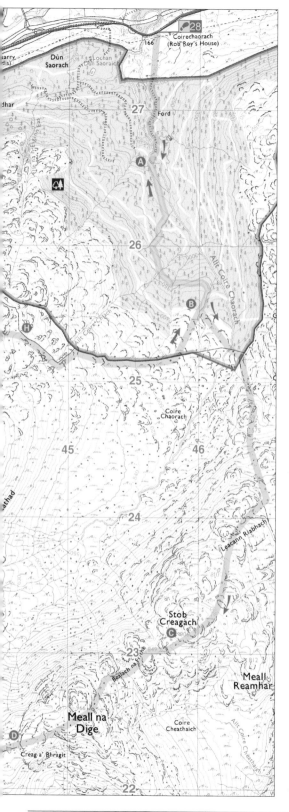

Cairngorm peaks. Ben More is the highest summit in Britain south of Strathtay and the biggest mountain in the Southern Highlands after Ben Lawers. Its name means, quite simply, 'big mountain'.

Leave by the north east ridge heading as though to Loch Tay. Keep to the left of a boulder-field (there is a cairn just before this) and at the rocky outcrop on the far side of it veer slightly left to find a narrow rocky path which runs along the northern edge of the ridge. This avoids several steep scrambles which would be encountered on the crest.

Continue to follow the ridge until you can see an easy way down to the deer fence (inevitably this means crossing rough ground). Turn right at the fence Ⓗ and follow it back towards the forest. At this stage of the outing this section may seem interminable, crossing acres of hummocky bog, but eventually you will reach an opening in the fence with a clear Land Rover track heading towards the gap in the forest from which you emerged Ⓑ, fresh as a daisy, some hours earlier. Once in the forest again follow the clear (albeit often waterlogged) path back to the start. ●

Further Information

The Law and Tradition as they affect Walking in Scotland

Walkers following the routes given in this book should not run into problems, but it is as well to know something about the law as it affects access, and also something of the traditions which can be quite different in Scotland from elsewhere in Britain. Most of this is common sense, observing the country code and having consideration for others and their activities, which may be their livelihood.

It is often said that there is no law of trespass in Scotland. In fact there is, but the trespass itself is not usually a criminal offence. You can be asked to leave any property, and technically 'reasonable force' may be used to obtain your compliance – though the term is not defined! You can be charged with causing damage due to the trespass, but this would be hard to establish if you were just walking on open, wild, hilly country where, whatever the law, in practice there

has been a long tradition of free access for recreational walking – something both the Scottish Landowners' Federation and the Mountaineering Council of Scotland do not want to see changed.

There are certain restrictions. Walkers should obey the country code and seasonal restrictions arising from lambing or stalking. Where there is any likelihood of such restrictions this is mentioned in the text and visitors are asked to comply. When camping, use a campsite. Camp fires should not be lit; they are a danger to moorland and forest, and really not necessary as lightweight and efficient stoves are now available.

Many of the walks in this book are on rights of way. The watchdog on rights of way in Scotland is the Scottish Rights of Way Society (SRWS), who maintain details on all established cases and will, if need be, contest attempted closures. They produce a booklet on the Scottish legal position *(Rights of Way, A Guide to the Law in Scotland, 1991)*, and their green signposts are a familiar sight by many footpaths and tracks, indicating the lines of historic routes.

The River Lochay from the old railway bridge

In Scotland rights of way are not marked on Ordnance Survey maps as is the case south of the border. It was not felt necessary to show these as such on the maps – a further reflection of the freedom to roam that is enjoyed in Scotland. So a path on a map is no indication of a right of way, and many paths and tracks of great use to walkers were built by estates as stalking paths or for private access. While you may traverse such paths, taking due care to avoid damage to property and the natural environment, you should obey restricted access notices and leave if asked to do so.

The only established rights of way are those where a court case has resulted in a legal judgment, but there are thousands of other 'claimed' rights of way. Local planning authorities have a duty to protect rights of way – no easy task with limited resources. Many attempts at closing claimed rights of way have been successfully contested in the courts by the Scottish Rights of Way Society and local authorities.

A dog on a lead or under control may also be taken on a right of way. There is little chance of meeting a free range solitary bull on any of the walks. Any herds seen are not likely to be dairy cattle, but all cows can be inquisitive and may approach walkers, especially if they have a dog. Dogs running among stock may be shot on the spot; this is not draconian legislation but a desperate attempt to stop sheep and lambs being harmed, driven to panic or lost, sometimes with fatal results. Any practical points or restrictions will be given in the text of each walk. If there is no comment it can be assumed that the route carries no real restrictions.

Scotland in fact likes to keep everything as natural as possible, so, for instance, waymarking is kept to a minimum (the Scottish Rights of Way Society signposts and Forest Walk markers are in un-obtrusive colours). In Scotland people are asked to 'walk softly in the wilderness, to take nothing except photographs, and leave nothing except footprints' – which is better than any law.

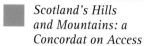

Scotland's Hills and Mountains: a Concordat on Access

This remarkable agreement was published early in 1996 and is likely to have considerable influence on walkers' rights in Scotland in the future. The signatories include organisations which have formerly been at odds - the Scottish Landowners' Federation and the Ramblers' Association, for example. However they joined with others to make the Access Forum (a full list of signatories is detailed below). The RSPB and the National Trust for Scotland did not sign the Concordat initially but it is hoped that they will support its principles.

The signatories of the Concordat are:

*Association of Deer Management Groups
Convention of Scottish Local Authorities
Mountaineering Council of Scotland
National Farmers' Union of Scotland
Ramblers' Association Scotland
Scottish Countryside Activities Council
Scottish Landowners' Federation
Scottish Natural Heritage
Scottish Sports Association
Scottish Sports Council*

They agreed that the basis of access to the hills for the purposes of informal recreation should be:

- Freedom of access exercised with responsibility and subject to reasonable constraints for management and conservation purposes.
- Acceptance by visitors of the needs of land management, and understanding of how this sustains the livelihood, culture and community interests of those who live and work in the hills.
- Acceptance by land managers of the public's expectation of having access to the hills.
- Acknowledgment of a common interest in the natural beauty and special qualities of Scotland's hills, and the need to work together for their protection and enhancement.

Further Information

The Forum point out that the success of the Concordat will depend on all who manage or visit the hills acting on these four principles. In addition, the parties to the Concordat will promote good practice in the form of:

- Courtesy and consideration at a personal level.
- A welcome to visitors.
- Making advice readily available on the ground or in advance.
- Better information about the uplands and hill land uses through environmental education.
- Respect by visitors for the welfare needs of livestock and wildlife.

Glossary of Gaelic Names

Most of the place names in this region are Gaelic in origin, and this list gives some of the more common elements, which will allow readers to understand otherwise meaningless words and appreciate the relationship between place names and landscape features. Place names often have variant spellings, and the more common of these are given here.

aber	mouth of loch, river
abhainn	river
allt	stream
auch, ach	field
bal, bail, baile	town, homestead
bàn	white, fair, pale
bealach	hill pass
beg, beag	small
ben, beinn	hill
bhuidhe	yellow
blar	plain
brae, braigh	upper slope, steepening
breac	speckled
cairn	pile of stones, often marking a summit
cam	crooked
càrn	cairn, cairn-shaped hill
caol, kyle	strait
ceann, ken, kin	head
cil, kil	church, cell
clach	stone
clachan	small village
cnoc	hill, knoll, knock
coille, killie	wood
corrie, coire, choire	mountain hollow
craig, creag	cliff, crag
crannog, crannag	man-made island
dàl, dail	field, flat
damh	stag
dearg	red
druim, drum	long ridge
dubh, dhu	black, dark
dùn	hill fort
eas	waterfall
eilean	island

eilidh	hind
eòin, eun	bird
fionn	white
fraoch	heather
gabhar, ghabhar, gobhar	goat
garbh	rough
geal	white
ghlas, glas	grey
gleann, glen	narrow, valley
gorm	blue, green
inbhir, inver	confluence
inch, inis, innis	island, meadow by river
lag, laggan	hollow
làrach	old site
làirig	pass
leac	slab
liath	grey
loch	lake
lochan	small loch
màm	pass, rise
maol	bald-shaped top
monadh	upland, moor
mór, mor(e)	big
odhar, odhair	dun-coloured
rhu, rubha	point
ruadh	red, brown
sgòr, sgòrr, sgùrr	pointed
sron	nose
stob	pointed
strath	valley (broader than glen)
tarsuinn	traverse, across
tom	hillock (rounded)
tòrr	hillock (more rugged)
tulloch, tulach	knoll
uisge	water, river

- Adherence to relevant codes and standards of good practice by visitors and land managers alike.
- Any local restrictions on access should be essential for the needs of management, should be fully explained, and be for the minimum period and area required.

Queries should be addressed to:
Access Forum Secretariat, c/o Recreation and Access Branch, Scottish Natural Heritage, 2 Anderson Place, Edinburgh EH6 5NP.

 ## Safety on the Hills

The Highland hills and lower but remote areas call for care and respect. The idyllic landscape of the tourist brochures can change rapidly into a world of gales, rain and mist, potentially lethal for those ill-equipped or lacking navigational skills. The Scottish hills in winter can be arctic in severity, and even in summer, snow can lash the summits. It is essential that the walker is aware of these hazards, which are discussed more fully in the introduction.

At the very least carry adequate wind- and waterproof outer garments, food and drink to spare, a basic first-aid kit, whistle,

Dunblane Cathedral

map and compass – and know how to use them. Wear boots. Plan within your capabilities. If going alone ensure you leave details of your proposed route. Heed local advice, listen to weather forecasts, and do not hesitate to modify plans if conditions deteriorate.

Some of the walks in this book venture into remote country and others climb high summits, and these expeditions should only be undertaken in good summer conditions. In winter they could well need the skills and experience of mountaineering rather than walking. In midwinter the hours of daylight are of course much curtailed, but given crisp, clear late winter days many of the shorter expeditions would be perfectly feasible, if the guidelines given are adhered to. *Think* is the only actual rule. Your life may depend on that. Seek to learn more about the Highlands and your part in them, and continue to develop your skills and broaden your experience.

Mountain Rescue

In case of emergency the standard procedure is to dial 999 and ask for the police who will assess and deal with the situation.

First, however, render first aid as required and make sure the casualty is made warm and comfortable. The distress signal (six flashes/whistle blasts, repeated at minute intervals) may bring help from other walkers in the area. Write down essential details: exact location (six-figure reference), time of accident, numbers involved, details of injuries, steps already taken; then despatch a messenger to phone the police.

If leaving the casualty alone, mark the site with an eye-catching object. Be patient; waiting for help can seem interminable.

Useful Organisations

Association for the Protection of Rural Scotland
Gladstone's Land, 3rd Floor,
483 Lawnmarket,
Edinburgh EH1 2NT
Tel. 0131 225 7012/3

Forestry Commission
Information Branch,
231 Corstorphine Road,
Edinburgh EH12 7AT.
Tel. 0131 334 0303
Cowal and Trossachs Forest District:
01877 382383
Loch Awe Forest District: 01546 602518

Historic Scotland
Longmore House,
Salisbury Place,
Edinburgh EH9 1SH.
Tel. 0131 668 8600

Loch Lomond Park Centre
Balmaha G63 0JQ.
Tel. 01360 870 470

Long Distance Walkers' Association
Bank House, High Street, Wrotham,
Sevenoaks, Kent TN15 7AE.
Tel. 01732 883705; www.ldwa.org.uk

Mountaineering Council of Scotland
The Old Granary, West Mill Street,
Perth PH1 5QP.
Tel. 01738 638227
www.mountaineering-scotland.org.uk

National Trust for Scotland
28 Charlotte Square,
Edinburgh EH2 4ET.
Tel. 0131 243 9300; www.nts.org.uk

Ordnance Survey
Romsey Road, Maybush,
Southampton SO16 4GU.
Tel. 08456 05 05 05 (Lo-call)

Ramblers' Association (main office)
2nd Floor, Camelford House,
87–90 Albert Embankment,
London SE1 7TW.
Tel. 020 7339 8500

Ramblers' Association (Scotland)
Kingfisher House, Auld Mart Business Park,
Milnathort, Kinross KY13 9DA.
Tel. 01577 861222

Loch Long and the Arrochar Alps from Doune Hill

Further Information

Royal Society for the Protection
of Birds Scotland HQ
Dunedin House, 25 Ravelston Terrace,
Edinburgh EH4 3TP.
Tel. 0131 311 6500
www.rspb.org.uk

Scottish Rural Property & Business
Association
Stuart House, Eskmills Business Park,
Musselburgh EH21 7PB.
Tel. 0131 653 5400
www.srpba.com

Scottish Natural Heritage
12 Hope Terrace,
Edinburgh EH9 2AS.
Tel. 0131 447 4784

Scottish Rights of Way & Access Society
24 Annandale Street,
Edinburgh EH7 4AN.
Tel. 0131 558 1222
www.scotways.com

Scottish Wildlife Trust
Cramond House, Kirk Cramond,
Cramond Glebe Road,
Edinburgh EH4 6NS.
Tel. 0131 312 7765
www.swt.org.uk

Scottish Youth Hostels Association
7 Glebe Crescent,
Stirling FK8 2JA.
Tel. 01786 891400
www.syha.org.uk

Tourist information:
Scottish Tourist Board
23 Ravelston Terrace,
Edinburgh EH4 3TP.
Tel. 0131 332 2433
www.visitscotland.com

Argyll, the Isles, Loch Lomond, Stirling
& Trossachs Tourist Board
Old Town Jail, St John Street,
Stirling FK8 1EA.
Tel. 01786 445222
E-mail: info@scottish.heartlands.com
www.visitscottishheartlands.com

*Local tourist information offices
(*not open all year):*
*Aberfoyle: 08707 200 604
Alva: 08707 200 605
*Ardgartan: 08707 200 606
Balloch: 08707 200 607
*Callander: 08707 200 628
*Drymen: 08707 200 611
*Dunblane: 08707 200 613
Falkirk: 08707 200 614
Glasgow: 0141 204 4400
*Helensburgh: 08707 200 615
*Killin: 08707 200 627
Stirling: 08707 200 620
*Tarbet-Loch Lomond: 08707 200 623
*Tyndrum: 08707 200 626

West Highland Way Ranger
Tel. 01389 722199
www.west-highland-way.co.uk

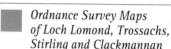

Ordnance Survey Maps of Loch Lomond, Trossachs, Stirling and Clackmannan

This area is covered by Ordnance Survey
1:50 000 ($1\frac{1}{4}$ inches to 1 mile or 2cm to
1km) scale Landranger map sheets 50, 51,
55, 56, 57, 58 and 64. These all-purpose
maps are packed with information to help
you explore the area. Viewpoints, picnic
sites, places of interest and caravan and
camping sites are shown, as well as public
rights-of-way information such as
footpaths and bridleways.

To examine the Loch Lomond and
Trossachs area in more detail, and
especially if you are planning walks,
Explorer maps 347, 348, 363, 364, 365,
366, 368, 369, 377 and 378 at 1:25 000
($2\frac{1}{2}$ inches to 1 mile or 4cm to 1km) are
ideal.

To get to Loch Lomond and the Trossachs
use the Ordnance Survey Travel Map-
Route Great Britain at 1:625 000 (1 inch to
10 miles or 4cm to 25km) scale or Ordnance
Survey Travel Map - Road 3 (Southern
Scotland and Northumberland) at 1:250 000
(1 inch to 4 miles or 1cm to 2.5km) scale.

Ordnance Survey maps and guides are
available from most booksellers, stationers
and newsagents.

www.totalwalking.co.uk

www.totalwalking.co.uk
is the official website of the Jarrold
Pathfinder and Short Walks guides. This
interactive website features a wealth of
information for walkers – from the latest
news on route diversions and advice from
professional walkers to product news, free
sample walks and promotional offers.